HOOP DRILLS

THE COACH'S GUIDE

HOOP DRILLS

THE COACH'S GUIDE

Vincent M. Mallozzi

FIREFLY BOOKS

A FIREFLY BOOK

First Published in Canada in 1998
by Firefly Books Ltd.
3680 Victoria Park Avenue
Willowdale, Ontario, Canada
M2H 3K1

Published in the United States in 1998
by Firefly Books (U.S.) Inc.
P.O. Box 1338, Ellicott Station
Buffalo, New York, USA
14205

Cataloguing in Publication Data

Mallozzi, Vinny
Hoop drills: the coach's guide

ISBN 1-55209-197-X

1. Basketball – Juvenile Literature. I. Title

GV885.1.M34 1998 j796.323 C97-932573-0

This book was designed and produced by
Quintet Publishing Limited
6 Blundell Street
London N7 9BH

Creative Director: Richard Dewing
Design: Deep Creative
Project Editor: Keith Ryan
Editor, Proofreader: Andrew Armitage, MFE Editorial
Photography: Paul Forrester, Britannia Studios
Additional Photography: London Towers Basketball Limited
(Pp. 19, 49, 69, 75, 76, 77, 101, 103, 105, 107, 108, 117)

**Special thanks to Rodney Alexander, Julian Morvan, Chris Bart-Williams,
Michael Redd and Derek Edwards for their help**

Typeset in Great Britain by
Central Southern Typesetters, Eastbourne
Manufactured in Singapore by Bright Arts Graphics Pte Ltd
Printed in Singapore by Star Standard Industries Pte. Ltd.

CONTENTS

Building the Right Foundation

BASKETBALL DRILLS ARE EXERCISES DESIGNED TO CONDITION PLAYERS, PREPARE THEM FOR THE GAME, AND KEEP THEM FOCUSED. THEY ARE PERFECT FOR BUILDING STAMINA, ACCURACY, AND TIMING. DRILLS ARE AT THE HEART OF VIRTUALLY EVERY SUCCESSFUL PLAYER'S GAME, AND NO ONE UNDERSTANDS THIS BETTER THAN COACHES, AT ALL LEVELS OF THE GAME. *HOOP DRILLS* IS A COLLECTION OF FAVORITE DRILLS USED BY SOME OF THE BEST AND MOST SUCCESSFUL BASKETBALL COACHES AROUND, IDEAL FOR PLAYERS AT EVERY STAGE OF THE GAME.

Fran Fraschilla, former coach of the St John's basketball team in New York, stresses two of the most important aspects of any basketball drill.

"First, there should be some element of pressure involved," he explains. "For example, I'll tell one of my players in practice that he has to make twelve shots in a minute. That puts an element of time pressure on that player, and some sort of fatigue or conditioning pressure." The St John's coach says the other important ingredient in basketball drills is overload.

"You must make a practice drill much harder than it would actually be in a game situation," says Fraschilla. "It must be more challenging in practice, the goals of the drill set much higher than the goals you're trying to achieve in the game."

Fraschilla, who has earned a reputation as a fiery, defensive-minded coach, states simply, "Drills help you improve the fundamentals of the game, and those fundamentals are the foundation of your game." Fraschilla points out that most of the drills practiced by college basketball coaches are used from the junior high school level straight up to the professional level. The coach knows that the majority of basketball players around the world will never make it to the pros, but he also knows that the very good ones, at any level, took their hoop drills seriously.

"You can't build a house without a solid foundation," says Fraschilla. "And you can't become a better player without sound knowledge of fundamentals."

For Starters

BASKETBALL COACHES AT ANY LEVEL WHO TAKE THE TIME TO CHAT X'S AND O'S WILL INEVITABLY MENTION THE WORD "FUNDAMENTALS" IN THEIR CONVERSATION. SOUND FUNDAMENTALS, A FIRM UNDERSTANDING OF THE BASIC ASPECTS OF THE GAME WHICH INCLUDE SHOOTING, PASSING AND DRIBBLING, MUST BE ESTABLISHED AT AN EARLY AGE IF A PLAYER HOPES TO ACHIEVE SUCCESS AND REACH MAXIMUM POTENTIAL THROUGHOUT HIS OR HER BASKETBALL LIFE. THERE AREN'T MANY "LATE BLOOMERS" OUT THERE WHO ARE DOMINATING ON THE PLAYGROUNDS OR THE HARDWOOD, AS MANY OF THE BETTER PLAYERS HAVE BEEN HONING THEIR SKILLS FROM THE TIME THEY WERE OLD ENOUGH TO LACE UP A PAIR OF SNEAKERS.

AT THE ELEMENTARY SCHOOL LEVEL AND IN MANY BASKETBALL CAMPS AROUND THE UNITED STATES, COACHES ARE TEACHING YOUNGSTERS THE FUNDAMENTALS OF THE GAME, AND IN THIS CHAPTER, A FEW OF THOSE COACHES SHARE SOME OF THE FUNDAMENTALS TO HELP TURN LITTLE SHOTS INTO BIG SHOTS.

Tex Winter, an assistant coach with the Michael Jordan-led Chicago Bulls, has 51 years of coaching experience at the Division I collegiate or professional level. The Bulls, who have won five NBA championships since the 1990–91 season, have the 75-year-old Winter to thank for much of the strategy that fills the pages of their playbook.

"Basketball surpasses all games in the matter of teamwork," says Winter. "Every player on the team receives the ball continually during an offensive movement within the scoring zone."

The following is a list of basketball terms as defined by Winter. Read and remember them as you go through each of the drills:

BALANCED FLOOR
An offensive formation displaying optimum spacing between players.

"BALL"
A call to alert defenders of a loose ball which is in play but not in possession of either team, or a tipped ball (the defensive deflection of an offensive pass or shot attempt) which the defense hopes will lead to a turnover.

BASEBALL PASS
A pass thrown like a baseball catcher, overhead, for a distance over 20 feet to key the fast break or hit a fly man (the player who has sprinted ahead of the field in an effort to make an uncontested layup).

BASKET CUT
After passing the ball from the wing, or the area of the floor extended from the foul line, the guard proceeds to cut, or break swiftly on an angle, to the basket.

"CHASE"
A defensive player follows an offensive player's hips and tailgates, or chases him through a series of picks.

CLOSE OUT
A controlled slide or proper lateral footwork by a defender to cover an offensive player.

"DENY"
A defensive play or stance that prevents an offensive player from receiving the ball.

"DOUBLE DOWN"
A defensive double-team on the post, the offensive area of the floor in and around the basket, where a player has positioned himself with his back to the basket for a catch or shoot sequence.

"HELP"
A defensive SOS, where one player rushes to the aid of a teammate who has blown his coverage.

HIGH POST
A post man positioned at or above the free-throw line.

"ISO"
A call to alert the team of an isolated offensive player.

ISOLATION
A term used to identify the area outside the three-point line where offensive player or players align themselves.

JUMP SWITCH
On switching, or swapping of players being guarded, a move into the path of the dribbler to force the player either to the baseline or stop the advance of the ball.

LOW POST
The post area below the free-throw line on the lane.

OPEN UP
A defensive drop-slide to an angle including ball and player.

OUTLET PASS
A pass, usually from a taller rebounder beneath the basket to a guard along the sideline, that initiates a fast break.

OVER-THE-TOP PASS
A high-arched pass, over the top of the defensive player attempting to front or deny a pass to a teammate – this is not a lob pass!

OVERLOAD
Occurs when an area of the floor is cleared either to the strong side or the weak side, the majority of players occupying one side.

"PICK"
A call for help from one defensive player to another, indicating an offensive player has stepped in front of, or screened, the player and forced an abrupt stop to his defensive pursuit.

"SEE THE BALL"
A call to alert the team or a player to get in a proper position to see the path of the ball clearly.

SMOTHER
A defensive surrounding of the ball, or an overplay to force traps, jump-balls, etc.

SPEED CUT
Break in to the basket on an angle under control, in an attempt to outrun an opponent to the basket or down-court.

SQUARE UP
A defensive stance, including bent knees, feet shoulder width apart, etc.

SQUARE UP TO THE BASKET
A catch-and-face-the-basket action that brings the player into a basic working position.

STRONG SIDE
The area of the floor where the basketball is present.

"SWITCH"
A call by one player alerting a teammate that two opposing players have switched or swapped the players they were originally guarding.

TOP OF THE CIRCLE
The area on top of the floor above the three-point line.

TRAILER
A post man or rebounder who follows or trails behind the fast break.

TRIPLE-THREAT POSITION
The position a player assumes with the ball where he can shoot, pass and cut, or dribble and drive to the basket.

TWO-HAND OVERHEAD PASS
A two-handed pass made with the arms extended, the wrist and fingers snapping only.

WEAK SIDE
The opposite side of floor from the ball's position.

WING SPOT
An area opposite the free-throw line extended to the top of the circle about three feet from the sideline.

FAST BREAK PASSING

Tommy Yahn, the head basketball coach at Intermediate School 183 in the South Bronx section of New York City, coaches many players at the elementary school level, ages 13 and under. At this stage, most players are getting their first taste of organized basketball.

"The little kids need to know the rules of the game and you have to give them a foundation," says Yahn, a former track and field star and football player at Penn State University. "At this level, teaching basketball requires a lot of patience and understanding – you have to understand what the physical limitations of your players are in relationship to the court."

One drill that Yahn enjoys teaching his young players is called the Fast Break Passing drill, which involves passing, shooting, dribbling, and running, and can be practiced in either a half-court or full-court set.

For this drill, Yahn sets his kids up in three lines of three players each. The middle line is standing just below the basket, but out of bounds, facing up-court. Players on the lines to the left and right of the middle line are also facing up-court.

At the whistle, the first players from the right and left lines, or Lines 1 and 3, start passing the ball to each other as they run full speed up toward the half-court line. The ball must not be dribbled, but passed swiftly back and forth between Lines 1 and 3 until those respective lines reach half-court. As Lines 1 and 3 pass the ball up-court, the middle

line, or Line 2, does not move. Once Lines 1 and 3 reach half-court, Line 2 will sprint into action, as the first player from Line 2 will sprint to the foul line. From here, the two offensive players will begin a two-on-one fast break back down the floor.

"Now, the offensive players are learning how to finish the fast break, and the defensive player is learning how to defend against the fast break," explains Yahn.

When the two offensive players are heading down-court, Yahn instructs the player with the ball to dribble toward the defender, forcing the defender to make a commitment and play the ball.

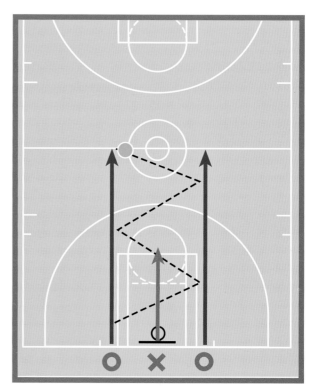

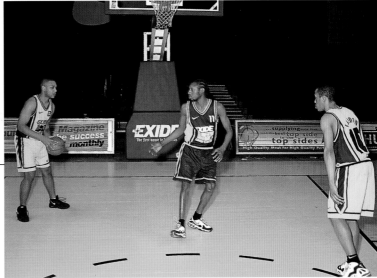

Once the players have done their run (see diagram), it all comes down to the two on one (see photos at right). This situation will arise time and again during a game. You have to learn how to deal with it early.

At the same time, the offensive player without the ball is instructed to run a wide pattern away from the ball while "filling the lane," or staying on an angle to the basket suitable for scoring once he receives a pass from the ball-handler.

When the first three players from each line have finished running the floor, players from all three lines rotate so that no one person is running the same pattern twice. This gives each player a chance to run the floor from two different perspectives, as well as giving each player a chance to play defense. Once each player fully learns this drill, Yahn will expand it to five lines (in this case, three offensive players will attack two defensive players), sometimes running those five lines the entire length of the floor.

"Remember, at this level, you want to teach the basics, but you also want to give the kids a drill that is fun to work," says Yahn. "You also want to get the kids learning how to condition, because the sooner they learn how to condition themselves properly, the easier the adjustment will be to the next level." The playground may seem easy for some, but wait until you hit the big leagues.

MOTION SPREAD

BALANCED FLOOR
AN OFFENSIVE FORMATION DISPLAYING
OPTIMUM SPACING BETWEEN PLAYERS.

A second drill that Tommy Yahn likes to run is called the Motion Spread drill, a version of the popular "give-and-go" play. To perform this drill, Yahn sets up two lines of six players each – one line on the corner of the baseline facing the far court, and the other group in a layup line on the same side of the floor, facing the near court.

At the whistle, the first player on the layup line heaves a quick chest pass into the corner. After releasing the ball, the player from the layup line cuts toward the basket on a 45-degree angle. After catching the initial pass, the player in the corner

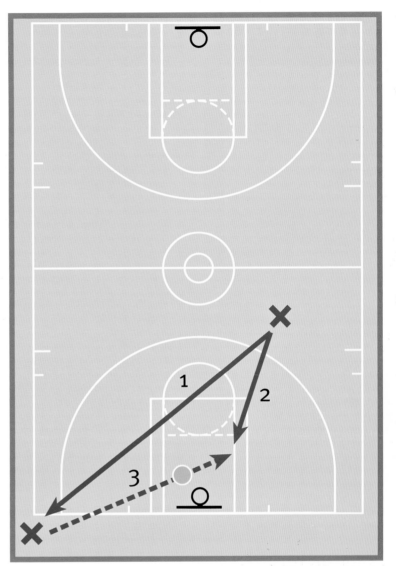

returns a bounce pass toward the basket to split the defense – "It's almost like the old Princeton backdoor play," says Yahn – where the cutting player will catch it on one hop, and lay the ball into the basket.

"This is a simple give-and-go from the baseline," says Yahn. "This drill is excellent for taking apart zone defenses. It forces the zone to come out and play you in the corner, opening up a big doughnut in the three-second area beneath the basket, where the cutter should catch the pass and have an easy, uncontested layup for a basket."

SIDE TO SIDE

Native New Yorker Richard Pee Wee Kirkland, a standout point guard at Norfolk State (Chicago) in the late 1960s, is now the head coach at the Dwight School in Manhattan, a private high school which Kirkland led to Independent League titles in 1997 and 1998. Kirkland, who was once drafted by the Chicago Bulls, is also the founder of the School of Skillz, a weekend basketball camp in Manhattan which offers instruction for hoop players six years of age and older.

"We teach the game from the neck up," Kirkland likes to say, "and that goes for my son too, and he's only two-and-a-half years old."

A phenomenal ball-handler in his heyday, Kirkland spends hours with his players on a ball-handling drill he calls Side to Side.

"This is the practice of dribbling laterally, which is really a form of advanced dribbling," says Kirkland. "When you see guys in the NBA with great cross-over dribble moves, guys like Allen Iverson, Tim Hardaway, and Stephon Marbury, well, all of those guys learned those moves because they learned how to dribble laterally." A simple but rewarding exercise, side-to-side dribbling, in its basic form, requires one player, in a park, in a gym, or in his own bedroom, with one basketball. Instead of dribbling straight, or in an up-and-down manner, the player will increase his ball-handling skills by using one hand to dribble the basketball, pushing the ball from the right to the left, and moving his dribbling hand behind the side of the ball he is pushing.

If, for example, a player is dribbling from right to left, he will push the ball laterally to his right, then reach over and across the ball and "catch" it by turning the palm of his right hand back toward his left leg.

Once the catch is made on the other side of the ball, the player then pushes or shifts the ball back to his left, catching the ball with the palm of his right hand facing his right leg.

"There's no stronger way to strengthen your left hand in basketball than to practice this drill," says Kirkland. Once Kirkland's players get used to dribbling side-to-side, he extends the drill by setting up bright red cones a few feet apart. Once his players go side to side, Kirkland has his players put the ball through their legs one time,

COACH'S CORNER

"THIS IS THE FUNDAMENTAL DRILL TO PREPARE PEOPLE FOR CROSS-OVER DRIBBLING."

RICHARD PEE WEE KIRKLAND, HEAD COACH, DWIGHT SCHOOL

catch the ball with a second hand, and go around a cone, and then again, and then again. "We make kids count 'one, two, through your legs, one two, through your legs'," says Kirkland.

By taking the drill to this level, Kirkland says his players are also practicing their "change of pace" dribble, or change of speed to throw an aggressive defense off balance.

"Now you're teaching the kid to dribble with both hands," says Kirkland. "And now, when it's all said and done, he won't be just a one-handed ballplayer anymore." A drill teaching the fundamentals such as this will apply to virtually all aspects of a player's game. It guarantees improved offensive skills when you hit the court in a real game.

Dribbling laterally is a skill acquired mainly through practice. The player in this sequence is taking the ball from left to right and back again with subtle dribbling touches, moving his hand from one side of the ball to the other to change its direction.

SUICIDE

As far as conditioning goes, Kirkland feels there is no better drill to build stamina than the dreaded Suicide drill. This drill, usually a form of coaching punishment for undisciplined players, requires an entire team of players to line up horizontally across the baseline at one end of the floor.

At the whistle, all players must run full speed to the first foul line, bend down to touch it, wheel around, and head back to the baseline. Upon reaching the baseline, the players bend again, touch it, wheel around again, and sprint to half-court, touching the half-court line, and then spinning back for a mad dash to the original baseline. After touching the baseline for a second time, all players continue back down the floor to touch the other free-throw line, zip back to the baseline, touch it a third time, and then, nearly out of breath, make the longest trek of the journey, all the way down to the other baseline – and all the way back.

"It's a lot of work," says Kirkland, "but it helps when you're trying to get a point across." It also increases stamina, essential for a winning game.

This may seem a simple drill but stamina is key in a game that lives for pressure. A quick glance at this diagram and you'll know the true meaning of stamina.

"BALL"
A CALL TO ALERT DEFENDERS OF A LOOSE BALL WHICH IS IN PLAY BUT NOT IN POSSESSION OF EITHER TEAM, OR A TIPPED BALL (THE DEFENSIVE DEFLECTION OF AN OFFENSIVE PASS OR SHOT ATTEMPT) WHICH THE DEFENSE HOPES WILL LEAD TO A TURNOVER.

LINE OF THE BALL

B ob Hurley Sr, whose son Bobby plays with the Sacramento Kings of the National Basketball Association, is one of the top high school hoop coaches in America. For the past 25 years, the senior Hurley has led St Anthony High School of Jersey City, New Jersey, to 19 State Championships. "I'm a drill nut," explains Hurley, who needs to win just one more State Championship to help St Anthony tie the national record. "But for all the drills that I use, I don't think I made up any of them myself. I've taken most of them and changed them around a little bit."

One of the drills Hurley loves to use in practice is a non-dribbling drill he calls Line of the Ball. This exercise requires six players – three offensive and three defensive.

At the whistle, the offensive unit will toss the ball in play, and attempt to work their way up the floor by passing, not dribbling, the basketball. "We encourage our guys to throw chest passes to each other," says Hurley. "Chest passes have become sort of a lost art."

For the offense, the main objective is to score a basket without committing a turnover. The defense must, as the drill implies, get in the line of the ball to make a steal or force a turnover.

"Here, the offense is working on passing and moving without the ball," says Hurley. "If the defense can get a steal, I reward them by allowing them to go down the other end of the court for a basket, and they can dribble if they want to."

Hurley says that this drill works best with a three-on-three setup because "if you use two-on-two, then you only have one defender off the ball, so it will not be as effective.

"Also, if you tried to go four-on-four, the floor simply becomes too clogged to run the exercise."

FOR STARTERS

FOUR-PASS FULL-COURT LAYUP

A second drill that Bob Hurley Sr offers is a lot more complicated to run, and is one of the most demanding in terms of stamina and conditioning. This drill, which Hurley calls the Four-pass Full-Court Layup drill, gives everyone on a full 12-player team the chance to work out.

Behind the baseline at one end of the floor, Hurley sets up four of his smallest players. At the nearest elbow (the area of the floor where the free-throw line and three-second lane meet), Hurley places two of his biggest players.

On the opposite end of the floor, Hurley places six other players in the exact same positions (again, four of his smallest players are placed behind the baseline, and two of his biggest are stationed at the nearest elbow). At either end of the floor, the first two players behind their respective baselines are each holding a ball, bringing a total of four basketballs to this exercise.

At the whistle, the first player from one baseline throws a pass out to the big player at the elbow. After receiving the pass, the big player will return the pass to the same player, who is running full-speed toward the other end of the floor.

After catching his first pass, the smallish player who broke from the baseline will whip another pass to the next big player waiting at the next

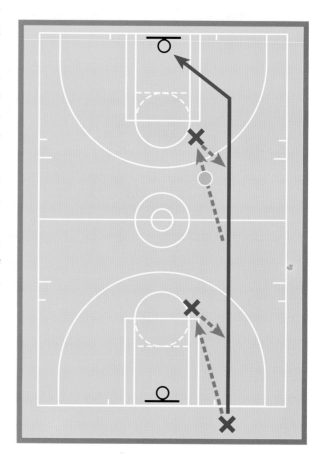

Running the length of the floor while giving and taking passes from elbow to elbow keeps a player's head up and legs moving at peak performance.

elbow. Continuing to run full-speed toward the net, the smaller player will get a second pass from the bigger player at the second elbow, and will either turn that pass into a two-step layup, a dribble and then a two-step layup, or a pull-up jumper.

"This is a great conditioning drill that requires full-court running," says Hurley. "For our big players, it is great for developing their hands and their passing skills, and for our smaller players, they are getting used to giving and going with the basketball and running in the open floor."

To give perpetual motion to this drill, Hurley allows the first player from one end of the floor to inbound the basketball immediately after the first player has done so. And, as soon as the first two players from each end of the floor inbound the ball and begin running the drill, the next two players, one from each side of the floor, will inbound the basketball to the second set of big players waiting at their respective elbows. When this drill is running at top speed, four basketballs and eight players are whipping around the floor, with four big players constantly catching and passing the ball.

"The important thing to remember here is that we are throwing a variety of passes, and doing a lot of other things like running and passing, at game speed," says Hurley. "This is a nonstop movement drill." Watch the ball on this one.

Pregame drills – some staged minutes before a game, like a layup line, and others staged days before, like a five-player weave and various shooting and passing drills – are essential in preparing a player mentally and physically for competition, and equally important in getting players' adrenaline flowing. Pregame drills often serve as a final strategic review, going over offensive and defensive concepts and getting focused on the task at hand. Some of the drills may be geared toward opposing individuals while others might be employed to disrupt the rhythm of an entire team.

Michele Sharp, former coach of Manhattan College's Division I women's team in New York, always tells her players that they should be going at game speed in pregame drills, so they are warmed up for the start of the game and ready for competition.

LAYUP LINES

This is a classic drill and a staple of the pregame warm-up. Players line up on both sides of the foul line. A player from Line 1 dribbles to the hoop and takes a layup, as a player from Line 2 moves in and rebounds the shot. The rebounded shot is passed off to the second player from Line 1, who is now moving in for a pass and the next layup attempt. This continues as each player gets a shot at the basket.

JUMPERS FROM THE WING

This follows the same set-up as the Layup Lines, but instead of going all the way to the hoop, each shooting player pulls up at a position extended from the foul line to launch an outside shot.

JUMPERS FROM THE FOUL LINE

Again, the setup is the same as the Layup Lines, but instead of going to the hoop, each player races to the foul line, stops on a dime, catches a pass, and launches from the free-throw line.

THE BACKBOARD TAP

The team lines up in two columns on each side of the free-throw line. The first player on the left dribbles toward the basket and tosses the ball off the backboard, where it is caught on first tap by the first player on the right, who taps the ball up again for the second player from the left. Each player taps the ball for the next player to follow and, after each tap, the player runs around and behind the approaching player from the other side to wait for his next turn.

Start your run as the player in front finishes his shot. Catch the ball on the rebound and aim for the backboard. Swerve behind the next incoming player and line up for another shot.

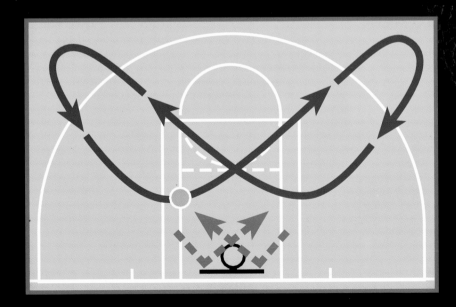

Getting a handle on things

DRIBBLING. THE SECRET WEAPON FOR GETTING OUT OF JAMS ON THE BASKETBALL COURT. THE SECRET WEAPON FOR ESTABLISHING THE BEST POSITION IN WHICH TO TAKE A SHOT, OR PASS THE BALL TO AN OPEN TEAMMATE. DRIBBLING IS CRUCIAL, AND THAT IS WHY COACHES AT EVERY LEVEL OF THE GAME INSTALL A VARIETY OF DRIBBLING SEQUENCES INTO THEIR PRACTICES. THOSE PATTERNS OF DRIBBLING HELP A PLAYER ACHIEVE HIS PRIME OBJECTIVE ON THE COURT. IN ONE CASE, A PLAYER MAY USE HIS DRIBBLE TO CHANGE DIRECTION ON THE FLOOR, OR USE ANOTHER DRIBBLE TO BACK UP HIS DEFENDER IN ORDER TO CREATE ENOUGH SPACE TO OPERATE. FORMER ST JOHN'S COACH FRAN FRASCHILLA AND FORMER MANHATTAN COLLEGE WOMEN'S COACH, MICHELE SHARP, HAVE PROVIDED A NUMBER OF HELPFUL DRIBBLING EXERCISES THEY INCORPORATE INTO THEIR RESPECTIVE WORKOUTS.

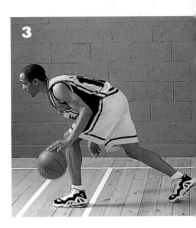

STRAIGHT AHEAD SPEED

Speed is one ingredient basketball simply cannot do without. The game is designed to keep the ball and players moving, from the shot clock to the three-second violation. Players must be able to take the ball where they want at the pace they want, maintaining control the whole way. Successful and effective dribbling drills have to contribute to a player's coordination, footwork, and awareness. These drills were designed to build up a player's abilities with ball handling and to increase confidence.

Two spots on the floor are marked, points A and B. A player takes the ball from point A and bursts ahead to point B, where he is clocked for speed. This helps build up speed and ball control during a fast break, which is essential during a game, and gives the player a better sense of accuracy in overall ball handling.

DRIBBLING BASICS

Keep your fingers stiff but supple as you dribble.
Use your fingertips, not your palm.

Keep the wrist action steady and maintain control on the way down as well as when the ball comes up to meet the hand.

Once you have mastered the coordination required for a steady firm dribble, you will find you can move the ball with even greater subtlety and control.

CROSS-OVER DRIBBLE

This is a clean, simple drill that brings home the very essentials of offensive play: stay low, stay in control and stay aware. A player dribbles with the right hand and accelerates to the right, until an opponent arrives. As soon as opponent lunges for the ball, the dribbler crosses the ball on a low dribble from right to left, leaving the defender chasing thin air. The dribbler, now using his left hand, can now dribble out of trouble.

This drill keeps the player moving and conscious of an opponent while keeping all options open: fast break for the basket, pass to another player or pull back for a shot.

COACH'S CORNER

"KEEP THE BALL LOW SO THAT A DEFENDER CAN'T REACH IN AND STEAL OR DEFLECT THE BALL, AND SHIFT YOUR WEIGHT TO CHANGE DIRECTION ON THE FLOOR."

MICHELE SHARP, MANHATTAN COLLEGE COACH, NEW YORK

CHANGE-OF-DIRECTION DRIBBLE

A deceptively simple drill, the Change-of-Direction dribble is all-important when confronting an opponent. It combines elements of Speed Dribble and Cross-Over Dribble and requires just as much accuracy. The player dribbles the ball from one side of the floor and shifts gears suddenly to head for the other side.

INSIDE-OUT DRIBBLE

A right-handed dribbler keeps the ball bouncing on the right, then takes the dribble to the middle of his body, but not beyond. From right to middle and back to the right side, repeatedly. Ball control is everything on the court. Simple tests of skill such as this will tell you a lot about your game.

STUTTER-STEP CHANGE

A player dribbles the ball as in Speed Dribble, timing the arrival of an approaching opponent in order to slow foot speed for an instant, forcing the defender to slow foot speed. The player then takes off again in full flight while the defender is still stuttering. This takes some skill and definite ball control as the player must pull up slightly while slowing down. Body language and eye contact can fool any opponent, so practice this drill seriously. Try to get your opponent off balance during the drill. This move requires substantial footwork, much more than meets the eye. Adjusting your speed and body language will fool a defender only if done with considerable skill, so make this drill a part of your practice sessions.

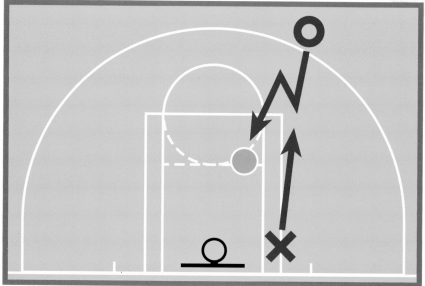

BACK-UP DRIBBLE

When an offensive player is being "trapped" by opposing players, he could lose the ball if he tried to dribble through the trap. Instead, the player must dribble up to the point of attack, then dribble back a few paces to create some space in front of the defender, enough to pass or shoot.

MARAVICH DRILLS

All ball-handling drills need an element of pressure to make them challenging, whether it is time, fatigue, or conditioning pressure. The Maravich Drills, named after the late "Pistol" Pete Maravich, one of the most phenomenal ball-handlers ever to play the game, are no exception. Fran Fraschilla, former coach of the St John's basketball team in New York, prefers these hand–eye coordination exercises above all others. The player wraps or dribbles the ball through and around his ankles in a figure of eight, and in one fluid motion, brings the ball up and begins wrapping it around the waist as fast as he can. Continuing this process, the player moves the ball up and begins wrapping it around his neck as fast as he can, clockwise and counterclockwise.

"This is an excellent drill, going one revolution at each spot," says Fraschilla. "It gives the player a oneness with the basketball."

Start dribbling the ball, with your right hand, in front of your body. Your legs and back should be bent and your knees about 18 inches apart. You should be poised and relaxed.

Dribble the ball to the right of your body, ready for the figure of eight. Control is as important as speed, so prepare to dribble the ball right around your leg.

Keep facing forward or to the side even when the ball is behind you, so that you keep your balance. As you start to dribble the ball forward again, move it into your left hand.

Keep your feet firm on the ground while you make the exchange. Dribble the ball forward and to the left.

Bring the ball around your left leg, just as you did around your right leg. Face forward and/or out to the right as you move the ball back into your right hand.

Each time you make a revolution, concentrate on control, as well as lower and faster dribbles.

As the ball returns to its original spot, move it upward, wrapping it around your knees, then your waist, upper torso, and neck.

COACH'S CORNER

"OVERLOAD THE DRILL. THE PRACTICE HAS TO BE MUCH HARDER THAN IT WOULD ACTUALLY BE IN A TEAM SITUATION, SO THE GOALS OF THE DRILL HAVE TO BE MUCH HIGHER THAN THE GOALS YOU ARE TRYING TO ACHIEVE IN THE GAME."

FRAN FRASCHILLA, ST JOHN'S UNIVERSITY, NEW YORK

THREE-PLAYER AND FIVE-PLAYER WEAVE

Players, three or five in total, steam down the floor, each taking a running lane. As they speed down the floor, the players run in figure-eight patterns, weaving between each other, a strategy intended to throw the opposition off balance and free up a player for an open shot.

TIP DRILLS

The players line up. The first player, holding the ball, tosses it off the backboard. Each player who follows must leap up, catching and tapping the ball off the board before landing, without letting the ball hit the floor. Each player keeps tapping off the board until the whistle blows.

AROUND THE WORLD

A player is passed the basketball from one corner of the floor, shoots, and works around the perimeter of the floor, taking another pass, shooting, taking another step around the horn before receiving yet another pass, shooting, and so on. The player moves around the horn, reaches one side of the floor, and then heads back to the other side of the floor. This drill is great practice for outside shooting, and a great way to work on a quick release, essential during a real game.

MACHINE-GUN PASSING

This drill, again provided by Fran Fraschilla, enhances passing skills, hand-eye coordination, and overall peripheral vision. It involves six to nine players and two basketballs. All the players except one form a semicircle, one of them holding a basketball. The other player, holding the other basketball, steps outside of the circle. On "Go!" or at the sound of the whistle, the player outside the circle, Player A, passes the ball quickly to one of the players standing inside the semicircle. As Player A releases the ball, the player holding the ball inside the semicircle fires a pass to Player A.

Player A catches the first pass and passes it off quickly to any person in the semicircle who does not have the other ball. As Player A releases the second pass, the player in the semicircle holding the ball passes again to Player A, and the blurring passes continue in and out of the circle, like a machine gun, in rapid-fire succession. As the players pass the ball to one another, each passer shouts out the name of the intended receiver, "John!" This gets the passer used to barking out the name of the teammate in traffic, and conversely, sharpens the reflex skills of the intended receiver.

If a group of players are bold enough, and, of course, skilled enough, they can attempt to increase the degree of difficulty for this exercise by adding another ball to the fun. In this case, two players would have to stand outside the semicircle and dish out passes while the players inside the circle fire the two other basketballs back in their direction.

COACH'S CORNER

"This is a major concentration exercise. It takes in many of the important elements that are a part of the passing game."

FRAN FRASCHILLA, ST JOHN'S UNIVERSITY, NEW YORK

Thinking Big – Offensive Drills for Larger Players

Y OU CAN'T TEACH HEIGHT. THAT IS HOW THE OLD BASKETBALL AXIOM GOES. BUT YOU CAN TEACH THE BIG PLAYERS THE FINER POINTS OF THE GAME. A QUALITY BIG PLAYER MOST OFTEN BECOMES THE DECIDING FACTOR DOWN THE STRETCH OF A CLOSE GAME, MAKING A CLUTCH, HIGH-PERCENTAGE SHOT FROM THE FIELD, OR SWATTING AWAY A SHOT ATTEMPT WHILE PLAYING DEFENSE. DAVE MAGARITY, TOM GREEN AND DENNIS O'DONNELL THINK BIG FOR THIS CHAPTER, SHARING THE DRILLS THEY USE TO GET THE MOST OUT OF THEIR FORWARDS AND CENTERS, THE PLAYERS WHO PLAY AND THINK ABOUT THE GAME A LOT DIFFERENTLY THAN DO SMALLER PLAYERS.

INDIVIDUAL POST DEVELOPMENT

Dave Magarity, the head coach at Marist College in Poughkeepsie, New York, has gained a reputation developing big players such as Rik Smits. Magarity's favorite drills for forwards and centers are: the Individual Post Development drill and the Two-Ball Low-Post drill.

"I tell my players that their concentration and discipline with this exercise will help them develop at the Division One collegiate level," says Magarity. "At the major college level they are playing against guys as big, as talented, and as strong as they are. The difference will be their discipline with the details and their ability to stay focused."

The big players form a line on the right side of the backboard. Each player has a ball in hand, and an additional ball is placed on the left side of the backboard. At the whistle, the first player advances to the backboard, springs upward, bangs the ball on the backboard, and comes down with the ball in hand. As soon as the player touches the ground, he immediately springs up again, banging the ball off the backboard. The player repeats this five times, and after the fifth bang, goes up strong and either lays the ball into the basket, or dunks it with authority (Magarity insists that the basket must be made or the player will have to repeat the drill).

After five bangs and a shot attempt, the player switches to the left side and repeats the same drill. When the first player switches from right to left, the second player on the line advances to the right side of the backboard, and begins his five bangs. A ballboy or teammate should feed the basketball to each new player. Magarity will increase the amount of repetitions to as many as 15 or 20 bangs.

COACH'S CORNER

"WE'RE TRYING TO GET OUR PLAYERS TO BECOME QUICKER JUMPERS OR MORE EXPLOSIVE JUMPERS FROM A REBOUNDING STANDPOINT. IT'S A GREAT STAMINA EXERCISE AND A GREAT CONDITIONER FOR THE LEGS."

DAVE MAGARITY, MARIST COLLEGE, POUGHKEEPSIE

TWO-BALL LOW-POST DRILLS

The second part of Magarity's exercise, the Two-Ball Low-Post drill, is designed to enhance a player's leaping ability and his low-post moves and quickness chasing loose balls. One ball is placed at the left box beneath the backboard, and another is placed at the right box beneath the backboard. Magarity forms a line of his big players near the free-throw line, and all of them wait for the whistle.

At the whistle, the first player sprints to the ball in the left box, picks it up, makes a "drop step" or approach to the basket and either lays the ball in the basket, or dunks it. As soon as he shoots the ball, he must rush immediately to the right box, pick up the ball, and drop step toward the hoop for another shot. The player continues this drill at a frenetic pace, usually for one full minute, before Magarity blows the whistle, which brings the next player into the drill. As the first player moves from left to right, and back again, a teammate along the baseline must continue to replace a basketball in each unoccupied box so that there is always a ball waiting to be picked up.

"What we are simulating here is quick reaction, the change from offense to defense, or from missing a basket to trying to scoop down real low for a loose ball, or some other transition scenario," says Magarity. "The player is staying low so that he is always ready to catch the next pass, or make a steal or perform some other type of reaction, so that there is no period of

COACH'S CORNER

"THE GOAL IS TO CONDITION PLAYERS MENTALLY NEVER TO RELAX, OR TO PREVENT THEM FROM HAVING THAT LULL WHERE AN OPPONENT MIGHT CATCH THEM OFF GUARD AND FORCE THEM INTO COMMITTING A FOUL."

DAVE MAGARITY, MARIST COLLEGE, POUGHKEEPSIE

letdown, and the player always stays sharp. It's an extremely tough drill."
By using one-minute intervals, instead of setting a number of repetitions, Magarity is able to tell which of his big players are working hard, and which ones aren't. If a player can make anywhere from 22 to 24 baskets, he is moving at an extremely quick pace. If a player can only produce about 15 or 16 baskets, "you know he's not working hard," says Magarity.

Magarity's players usually perform this part of the drill three days out of a five-day practice cycle. In between those three days, he will have his players work on the Individual Post Development drill.

SPECIALTY SESSION DRILLS

Tom Green has been the head basketball coach at Fairleigh Dickinson University in New Jersey for the past 15 years. Coach Green spends four days a week working with his taller players, and teaching them a variety of moves in the low-post area around the basket.

"We do what we call a Specialty Session," says Green. "This session is a series of five fundamental drills that are geared specifically toward the big guys."

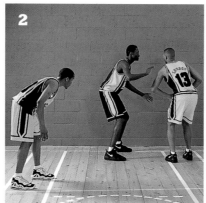

PART 1:

The first part of the Specialty Session requires a player setting up in the low-post area and practicing the Drop Step. The player is taught to hold one arm up in an L-shaped fashion to hold off the defender. While screening the defender, the player holds out his "target" hand, into which his teammate will attempt to pass the ball.

The position of the player's arms depends on the side of the floor he's on. If the player is on the left block, his left hand is his target hand, and his right hand is the screen.

From here, the player will attempt to drop step to the basket. Assuming the drop step is coming from the left side of the basket, the player will wheel on his (right) pivot or plant foot, while the pass is in the air, drop or swing his left foot closer toward the basket, and wait for a pass to be thrown into his target hand, where he should be able to convert a basket.

PART 2:

The second part involves the big player getting off a shot while the defender is "hanging all over his back."

"One of the lost arts in basketball is pivoting and facing the basket," says Green. "Everybody wants to make a move with their back to the basket, but we try and teach them to face the basket."

From either side of the floor, a player who has his back to an aggressive defender, must pivot at a 180-degree angle, face or "square up" to the basket, and get off a shot.

"Some kids that I get at the college level are just used to pivoting one way," says Green. "We just simply teach them to pivot from either side, and just shoot."

PART 3:

This part of Green's drill is a continuation of PART 2. Here, after the catch is made, and the player pivots at a 180-degree angle toward the basket, he must add a "pump fake" to his move. By pump-faking, or making a defender believe that an initial quick shot will be taken, the shooter is sometimes able to lure a defender off his feet or throw him off balance, giving the shooter an even better look at the basket.

PART 4:

At this point, a player will catch, pivot, pump-fake and then cross over. "If we pivot with our right foot to face up the basket from the left block, we will pick our left leg up, step across with one dribble toward the middle, and look for a shot."

PART 5:

The last part of Green's drill is a tribute to Jack Sikma, a former NBA player who starred with the Seattle SuperSonics and the Milwaukee Bucks.

The Sikma Move, as Green calls it, is what is more commonly referred to as a "reverse pivot" or "inside pivot."

To illustrate this move, a player who is operating on the left block and receives a pass will not spin or pivot toward the basket with his left foot wheeling forward. Instead, he will pivot or plant with his left foot, and, as opposed to going left, will lean right toward the middle of the lane, pivoting clockwise in an effort to create space away from the defender and get off a better shot.

"Jack Sikma was the only guy I saw use that move consistently throughout his career," says Green. "He didn't have a lot of moves, but he had that one."

TIP-IN

As far as his big players are concerned, Dennis O'Donnell, the head coach at St Thomas Aquinas College in Sparkill, New York, whips them into shape with a four-part drill he got from former New York Knicks coach Hubie Brown, called the Tip-In drill.

First, O'Donnell has his big players lined up at the right side of the basket. At the whistle, the first player, taking off from the foul line, tosses the ball off the backboard using his left hand, and when the ball comes off the board, that player will tip it into the basket using his right hand. After each tip-in, the big player next in line will be fed a basketball from a player or team manager and perform the same task.

In the second phase of this drill, O'Donnell will have a line of his big players start from the right side of the basket, toss the ball off the backboard using their right hand, rebound the ball with two hands – "You must keep the ball held over your head with two hands so that no one can try to swat it away from you," says O'Donnell – then go straight back up and dunk it. O'Donnell refers to this particular exercise as Pogo-ing.

"Everything we do, we start on the right side and go left," says O'Donnell. "But remember, everything we do with one hand, we'll practice with our other hand."

In the third phase of this exercise, O'Donnell has his big players lined up again at the right side of the foul line. This time, the first big player on line tosses the ball off the backboard with his left hand, rebounds the ball with both hands, comes down to the floor, pump-fakes against a real or imaginary defender, and then goes back up and dunks the ball.

In the final phase, the big player, starting from the right side, will again throw the ball off the backboard with his left hand, rebound the ball with both hands, come down, pretend that a big defender has taken away his angle to the basket, make one strong dribble toward his left, and then lay the ball in the basket from the left side of the backboard.

"For the Tip-In drills, we'll use imaginary defenders," says O'Donnell. "But for the power stuff, we'll usually have real defenders in there."

PLANT AND GO

Another one of Dennis O'Donnell's big-player drills requires neither an imaginary defender nor a real one. Sometimes, however, the drill does require a tackle dummy similar to the one used to block National Football League players during strength and conditioning workouts.

To set up the basic drill, O'Donnell places one ball on the right block and another on the left block. One big player will be stationed in the middle of the lane, another on the left block, and yet another on the right block. To add a physical dimension to the drill, a fourth big player can be positioned beneath the basket holding the plastic or rubber dummy.

At the whistle, the offensive player in the middle of the lane, facing the basket, will go for the ball on the right block. That player will then plant his left foot, bend over, grab the ball, pull it in tightly toward his chest, and then go for a shot or lay the ball in the basket.

If he has decided to include the dummy in the drill, O'Donnell will have his defensive player beneath the basket hold the dummy out in a defensive stance. When the big player on offense attempts to go in for his layup, the dummy will attack him, or make contact. The big players on the left and right blocks are merely in this drill to keep reloading balls on the blocks so that the drill can constantly be repeated by the main player.

"All you're doing is teaching the guy to plant his feet, tuck the ball to his chest so nobody slaps it away from him, and then go hard to the hole," says O'Donnell. "You're always planting your interior foot, so if you're on the right block, you want to plant your left foot, and on the left block, you want to plant your right foot." If you want to improve your speed and accuracy, this drill is it.

The basic Plant and Go – the player moves to the right-hand ball (1), plants his left foot and picks up the ball (2), pivots to face the basket in a triple-threat position (3), and takes a shot (4), then continues the drill. The diagram shows the set-up as it would appear with a tackling dummy near the basket.

On the Attack – Overall offensive drills

Whenever you see a point guard flash a hand signal to his teammates or hear a coach bark out a strange word or unfamiliar phrase to his troops from along the sideline, a pre-planned offensive play is underway. A good offensive attack requires concentration, discipline, hustle and the timely ability to execute carefully diagrammed plays. In this chapter, some of the greatest coaches in history share their favorite offensive drills, the ones they spent years of perspiration working on, the ones that helped turn their teams into champions or perennial contenders.

REPEATS

Jay Wright, the head basketball coach at Hofstra University on Long Island, New York, is a rising star in basketball coaching and has contributed two drills to this book: the Circle Rebound drill (see Chapter 6), and this unique exercise, called Repeats.

Repeats uses two players, each holding a ball, and two coaches. "The purpose of this drill is to work on your offensive skills within an offensive pattern," says Wright. "We work specifically on setting screens, using screens and on our offensive moves."

At the whistle, Player A starts at the top of the key holding the ball, and Player B stands on the right wing (extended from the right side of the foul line) without the ball. One coach is foul-line extended on the left wing, and the other coach, also holding a ball, is standing next to him.

Player A passes the ball to one coach. Player A cuts straight to the basket, then breaks in a V-like formation to set a screen for Player B.

Player A sets his pick, or screen, for Player B. One coach now passes the ball to Player B. Player A, after setting the pick, now pops out to the wing, or foul-line extended. Player B passes the ball to Player A, who now shoots off that pass. After making his pass to Player A, Player B makes a hard cut to the basket, and he receives a pass from the other coach.

"You can do whatever you want with this drill," says Wright. "You can work in ball fakes, back cuts, cross-over dribbles, whatever. But the most important thing to remember is to incorporate any of these moves in the context of a particular offense."

This diagram shows the initial stage of the drill, taking Player A from the top of the key to the screen for Player B.

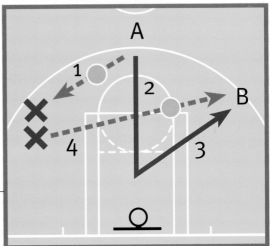

ONE-ON-ONE FROM THE SIDE

Lou Carnesecca, a legendary professional and college coach, piloted the New York Nets of the old American Basketball Association before taking over the reins at St John's University in Queens, New York. Carnesecca's Redmen teams – his 1985 squad reached the NCAA Final Four – produced a number of quality professional players over the years, including Chris Mullin and Mark Jackson of the Indiana Pacers, Malik Sealy of the Detroit Pistons, Jayson Williams of the New Jersey Nets, and Bill Wennington of the Chicago Bulls.

Despite his retirement at St John's, Carnesecca continues to tour internationally with collegiate All-Star teams each summer, and he still uses the same practice drills that made him a household name in the world of roundball.

Carnesecca's favorite drill of all time is one he calls One-on-One from the Side. According to Carnesecca, this exercise, which requires three players, is an "all-composite offensive and defensive drill."

In setting up this drill, Carnesecca places one player at the top of the 3-point circle holding the ball. A second player is on the right side of the floor, foul-line extended to the 3-point circle, and a third player is extended from the foul line on the opposite side. Three groups of three players each are waiting their turn out of bounds.

At the whistle, Player A, who is holding the ball, passes to his right to Player B. Player A then runs behind Player B, as if he will get a hand-off back from Player B. Meanwhile, Player C, on the left side of the floor, sprints into the area just above the foul line. Player B fakes a hand-off to Player A,

passes the ball to Player C, then runs behind Player C as if he will take a hand-off pass. After a faked hand-off, Player C passes the ball to Player A, who is now standing at the right side of the free-throw line extended, and Player B wraps around Player C and sprints to the middle of the 3-second lane into a defensive position. Meanwhile, Player C races back to Player A and goes into his own defensive stance.

"What you have now is Player C playing defense against Player A with Player B in a defensive position," says Carnesecca. "We're moving with the ball and without the ball – it's an all-composite drill." From this point, Player A has the option of making whatever one-on-one move he can make in an attempt to score a basket.

"Let's say that Player A chooses not to pull up for a jumper but to drive past Player C," says Carnesecca. "Well, in that case, here comes Player B to help out."

Once Player A gets off a shot, he hopes to score. If he doesn't, the rebounder of the basketball becomes the offensive player, and that player must try to score against the other two players, both of whom are now on defense.

"We just keep banging the ball until somebody scores, and there are no fouls called while play is going on," says Carnesecca, who ran this drill every day in practice for about 15 minutes each session.

"This is an offensive-defensive drill where the players just keep going until the ball goes into the basket." The quick offensive-defensive transitions of this drill will keep players on their toes and prepare them for real game situations.

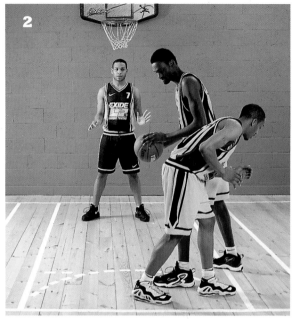

COACH'S CORNER

"IN THIS DRILL, WE'RE TEACHING ALL THE FUNDAMENTALS OF THE GAME. WE'RE TEACHING HOW TO MOVE WITHOUT THE BALL, FAKE HAND-OFFS, SQUARE UP TO THE BASKET TO SHOOT AND PLAY DEFENSE."

LOU CARNESECCA, FORMER COACH OF ST JOHN'S UNIVERSITY, QUEENS

BOX DRILL

Tim Welsh, former head basketball coach at Iona College in New Rochelle, New York (now head basketball coach for Providence College), and his top assistant, Jeff Ruland, a former NBA player, now head coach at Iona, often used the Box Drill in their practices. The Box Drill is basically an individual instruction exercise which allows a player to work on a variety of options.

"The purpose of this drill is to improve a player's triple-threat fundamentals and allow a player to get by his defender with proper footwork," says Welsh. "A triple-threat position is a position where a player can shoot, drive, or pass depending on what his defender is doing."

To begin the Box Drill, a player is positioned on the baseline holding a basketball. A spot is designated at the 3-point line or at the top of the key area. At the whistle, the player then rolls the ball out in front of him, and races to retrieve it at either one of the designated areas.

The player must catch up to the ball and grab it while jump-stopping, which means leaving the floor with both feet before coming to a complete landing. After the jump-stop, the player's back should be toward the baseline. At this point, the player, now on offense, should pivot, or wheel around, using either foot. After the player establishes a pivot foot, he is now in the triple-threat position.

Next, the player should fix both eyes on the rim of the basket, and give a head fake to a real or imaginary opponent. By offering a head fake, the player holding the basketball allows the defender to believe that he is heading in the direction in which he has leaned his head forward. If a defender should "buy" the fake, by leaping straight into the air, the player will wait for the defender to land on his two feet, and then time his rise to take an uncontested shot at the basket, or put the ball on the floor and drive past a defender before he gets to his feet.

After practicing a head fake, the player then offers a ball fake by jutting the ball out in any direction. If the defender should be tricked into believing that the player's body will follow in the path that the ball seems to be heading, then the player can quickly pull back the ball, put it on the floor and drive around the defender. Also, in a game situation, if the defender has been tricked off

balance, the offensive player might choose to pass the ball to an open teammate.

"Remember," says Welsh, "after you get into a triple-threat position, you must know which foot to push off. If your pivot foot is your right foot, you should be stepping with your left foot past the defender while pushing the ball in front of you to drive for a layup."

In the Box Drill, a player rolls a basketball to a spot on the floor where he "jump stops" to the ball (1), pivots to face the basket (2), then head fakes (3) and ball fakes (4) against an imaginary defender before heading to the basket for a shot (5).

BOTH WELSH AND RULAND OFFER THESE VARIATIONS TO THE BOX DRILL:

- Practice your footwork by pivoting with both feet. This will make you more comfortable with driving to the basket using either foot first during play.

- Start the Box Drill past the 3-point line. This will allow the offensive player to become more familiar with operating further from the basket during a game.

- Use a chair as the first defender, but then insert a real defender behind the chair. The real defender must try to block your shot after you get by the chair.

- Instead of always attempting a layup, take one dribble, come to a jump-stop again, and pull up for a shot.

- Use the Box Drill on both the left and right sides of the floor, as coaches often plan attacks from either side during a game.

- Practice the Box Drill from the wing – a position extended from the foul line – or baseline areas on both sides of the floor.

AND TWOS

Pete Carril, now an assistant coach with the Sacramento Kings of the National Basketball Association, is simply a coaching genius. Before joining the Kings, Carril enjoyed a long, successful tenure as head coach at Princeton University in New Jersey, where his smart coaching helped the usually undermanned Tigers tame much more dangerous opponents. When asked to share his favorite hoop drill, Carril did not hesitate: "The name of my all-time favorite drill is 'And Twos'," says Carril. "I picked this drill up in 1952, when I went to watch a New York Knicks practice, and Joe Lapchick was the coach.

"I never saw guys having so much fun while working so hard," says Carril. "They just loved doing this drill." Carril's favorite drill is fairly simple to run, but reaps tremendous rewards. It requires groups of five players each spreading out across one of the two baselines. At the whistle, the basketball is tossed

into play to the player at the extreme right on the baseline, and in unison, all five players pick a running lane, and start running up the court.

As the players head up-court, the player on the extreme right tosses the ball to a player in the middle of the floor, which will be either the second or third player from the left. Never, says Carril, should the player on the extreme right side throw the ball to the player on his immediate left, nor should any player pass the ball to a teammate who is running in the very next lane. In fact, each pass should occur with at least two lanes of distance between the passer and the receiver.

Keeping these distance rules in mind, the ball should then be tossed back and forth accordingly. For example, if the player on the far right side of the floor – let's call him Player A – passes to the player who is two lanes away on his left (Player C), then Player C will likely pass the ball to the far left side, in this case Player E.

The key to this drill: As the players steam up-court, no one is allowed to dribble. However, they must catch and pass the ball without committing a violation. As the players work their way toward the basket, one of them must catch the last pass and convert a layup. Once the layup is made, the

players will rebound the ball, reverse direction, and head down the other end of the floor in similar fashion. Carril says he usually ran three groups of five for eight to ten minutes each practice session.

"You can't walk with the ball; you can't drop it or commit any violation of any kind," says Carril. "The way I ran it is my players had to run up and down four times and make three layups. For every layup they missed, they'd have to run two more, and that's real tough – that's why I called the drill 'And Twos'.

"If you bounce the ball, then you're defeating the purpose," Carril adds. "It's a great ball-handling drill because you're always passing and catching, passing and catching. It also teaches the value of teamwork and adds a lot of camaraderie to the group."

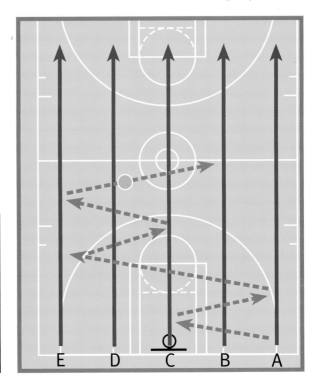

COACH'S CORNER

"THIS DRILL MAKES YOU KEEP YOUR HEAD UP, LOOK AHEAD, AND THROW IT TO THE FIRST OPEN GUY YOU SEE."

PETE CARRIL, ASSISTANT COACH, SACRAMENTO KINGS

THE DRIVE DRILL

At Princeton, Pete Carril made the Tigers famous for a play called the Backdoor Cut. A two-player offensive play, a successful backdoor cut requires one offensive player to catch the defense either napping or being overaggressive. If that is the case, then the offensive player will bolt past his defender. Once past his defender, the offensive player, or backdoor cutter, will take a bounce pass or aerial pass from his teammate, and sneakily whisk to the basket for a layup.

To enhance the skills required to pull off the Backdoor Cut, Carril practiced an exercise called the Drive Drill.

This drill required two players, one standing at the top of the key dribbling the basketball, and the other standing to his left or right, extended from the foul line on either side. The player at the top of the key (Player A), would dribble toward the player extended at the foul line. When the two players meet, the player wanting to receive the ball (Player B), attempts to sneak around the dribbler and take a hand-off pass, much the way a running back in football takes a hand-off from his quarterback. If the hand-off is successful, Player A steps in between Player B and the defender to act as a shield, or in basketball terms, he becomes the "screener."

While the receiver stays free of the defense for a moment behind the screener, he has an option of shooting the basketball.

The key to the backdoor cut, which is practiced in the Drive Drill, is that moment when quarterback and receiver meet. If the defender is overplaying Player B, or guarding him much too closely in an attempt to prevent the hand-off, then Player B does not go toward the ball, but fakes that movement and slips past his defender to the basket without the ball in hand. If Player B breaks free, Player A will get him a pass for a wide-open layup. If, at the meeting point, a defender is too slow to move his feet, then Player B might have an easy opportunity to slip past him for a backdoor cut without ever faking any move toward Player A.

"The tendency is for defenders to want to gravitate toward the path of the ball all the time," says Carril. "Both players must read the defense properly, and remember, do not go toward the ball when you're being overplayed. Also, if you can sense that the guy defending you, at any time, loses sight of you, then you can go backdoor." To perfect this drill, Carril starts his players off against imaginary defenders and then adds real defenders for greater challenge.

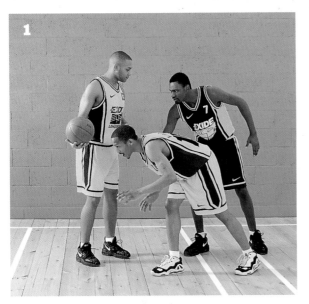

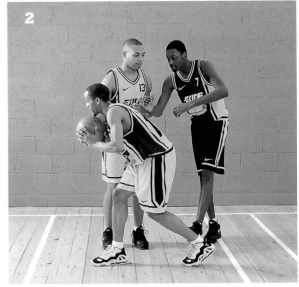

COACH'S CORNER

"AFTER THE TWO OFFENSIVE PLAYERS LEARN ALL THE POSSIBILITIES OF WHAT THEY CAN DO PLAYING THAT TWO-MAN GAME, THEN YOU ADD THE DEFENSE IN THERE SO THAT YOUR PLAYERS CAN START TO READ WHAT YOU HAD JUST TAUGHT THEM."

PETE CARRIL, ASSISTANT COACH,
SACRAMENTO KINGS

LONG PASS DRILL

No one in the history of the National Basketball Association won more championships than Red Auerbach of the Boston Celtics. From 1946 to 1966, Auerbach compiled a record of 938 victories against 479 losses for a 66.2 winning percentage, raising nine championship flags along the way.

Auerbach, who was voted the "Greatest Coach in the History of the NBA" by the Professional Basketball Writers' Association of America in 1980, put some of the legendary players in the history of the sport – from Bill Russell to Larry Bird – through numerous hoop drills. For this project, Auerbach shared one of his favorite drills, a fundamental exercise he called the Long Pass Drill. "I ran this drill every day in practice for twenty years," says Auerbach.

In this drill, Auerbach would split his team in half, placing six or seven players in a single line along the sideline on one end of the floor, and placing the other half of his team along the sideline on the opposite end of the floor, also in single line.

On one line, the first player is holding the basketball. At the whistle, the first player on the opposite end of the floor breaks toward the basket, and the player holding the ball launches a long "baseball" pass down the floor, simulating a fast-break pass thrown clear over the entire defense.

After catching the pass, the receiver must make a layup, grab his own rebound, whirl around, and fire an identical pass to the player who had just thrown him the ball. Once the second layup is made, that player will rebound his own shot, and continue the rapid pace of the drill by whirling, and launching a long pass to the next breaking player at the other end of the floor. From there, the drill continues "for about five or six minutes," says Auerbach, "depending on how long I wanted to work them that day.

"This drill helped discipline players in lifting their heads up before they released a pass, and leading a player with a pass," says Auerbach. "On the other end, it taught players how to catch a difficult pass in stride and make a layup, which is not as easy as it looks when you're going full speed."

Auerbach, whose fabled teams featured some of the greatest shooters of all time, says he loved to split his players up beneath different baskets in groups of two and three to compete head to head against each other, a free-wheeling way to develop one-on-one moves. "I used to let them play Twenty-One," says Auerbach, referring to the street game in which every player plays for himself, and shoots up to three free throws after every made basket. In this game, the first player to reach 21 points is the winner.

Hoping that all coaches everywhere might be reading these words, the legendary Auerbach offered some valuable advice on the subject of shooting drills: "I would always let my players do most of their shooting drills at the end of practice, when they were already exhausted," says Auerbach. "Remember, a lot of guys look good shooting in practice, but when a game comes, they don't shoot as well because they can't adjust to shooting when tired." Remember, stamina and quick thinking can win ball games.

FOUR CORNERS

anice Quinn, the head coach of the New York University women's basketball team, led the Violets to a Division III Championship in 1996–97. For this project, Quinn shared an all-purpose drill she calls Four Corners, an exercise that has drawn considerable praise from coaches and players.

"The reason why we get such great feedback from this drill is that it gets everyone involved and very active," says Quinn. "When high school coaches come and watch us play, the first thing many of them tell us is, 'Wow, where did you get that warm-up!' "

To set up this drill, Quinn uses all 16 of her players operating within a half-court set. Groups of four players each are in a single-line formation in each of the four corners that make up the half-court. In other words, four players are standing in a line at the southeast corner of the court along the mid-court line. Across from them on the left are four players in a line at the southwest corner of the court, also along the mid-court line. Both of these lines are parallel to the mid-court line, facing each other.

On the northeast corner of the floor, along the baseline, four more players are standing in line, facing mid-court. On the northwest corner of the floor, also along the baseline, four more players are standing, facing the players standing at the northeast corner.

To simplify matters, let's call the southwest group Line 1, the southeast group Line 2, the northeast group Line 3, and the northwest group Line 4.

To begin this drill, the player at the front of the southwest line, or Line 1, is holding the ball. At the whistle, the player will throw a chest pass across to the first player waiting in Line 2.

Once the person from Line 2 catches the ball, she will pivot to her right and throw another chest pass to the first player in the northeast corner on the baseline, or Line 3. The player who has caught the ball in Line 3 pivots to her right, and makes a cross-court chest pass to the first person in the northwest corner, or Line 4.

"So the ball has now been whipped around counterclockwise from Line 1 to 2 to 3 to 4," says Quinn. "This is the path the ball will follow, and now we run our players around in a similar path."

The person who initially passed the ball from Line 1 to Line 2 to start the drill, follows the flight of the ball and sprints behind the passer from Line 2 as the lead player from Line 2 is passing the ball off to Line 3. After catching the pass, the lead player in Line 3 pivots to her right, and, as the initial passer is passing behind her, fires a pass to the lead player from Line 4. As the lead player from Line 4 catches the next pass, the initial passer who started the drill from Line 1, is now cutting on a 45-degree angle toward the basket.

As the initial passer cuts toward the basket, the lead player from Line 4 who has just caught the pass will return a bounce pass to the initial passer, who will catch the bounce pass and attempt a layup.

"Part of this drill is that you have to meet your pass," says Quinn. "Part of this drill also works on footwork. The person from Line 3, for example, actually takes one quick little stride, or two strides in toward the basket, plants her right foot, and drives herself up to the person who has the ball in Line 2 to meet the pass. By doing that, the player from Line 3 has made the distance for the player traveling from Line 1 a shorter distance."

From here, the person who has taken the layup steps off the court, and continues her forward motion to the right side of the court, and takes up a position as an inbound-passer. The player who threw the bounce pass will move beneath the rim to serve as the rebounder after the attempted layup. The rebounder, now on the court, will then throw an outlet pass to the inbound (the player who took the initial layup), who is standing out of bounds behind the baseline.

"Meeting the pass is critical," says Quinn. "You have to have precise timing on your cuts, and if you miss the layup, you screwed up the whole drill."

Once the inbounder (the player who threw the first pass and ended up cutting to the hoop for the first layup) receives a pass back from the rebounder, she throws an outlet pass back to the next player waiting in Line 1, and the drill starts going around and around in one fluid, continuous motion.

"In order to keep the continuity of this drill, everyone must know where they are going like the back of their hand," explains Quinn.

After throwing the outlet back to Line 1 to start the drill again, the inbound must step in back of Line 4. The player who was originally first in Line 2 follows out of the way and falls in back of Line 1. The person in line 3, who had stepped into the lane and met the pass from Line 2, steps out of the way after

passing to Line 4 and fills in at the back of Line 2. The player in Line 4, who makes the bounce pass for the layup, steps off the court – after rebounding the layup and passing back to the inbound – and steps back of Line 3.

"We do this drill with up to three or four balls simultaneously," says Quinn. "We usually put the second ball into play after the second pass is made, so when the person from Line 3 catches the ball, the next person from Line 1 will put the next ball in play. With sixteen players, four in each line, we get three balls going." Quinn, who runs this exercise for a maximum of four or five minutes per practice, pointed out the various skills that are associated with this drill and what you can expect to develop by following this drill during your own practice sessions.

"Concentration is a must, and timing is critical," she says. "Next would be quality and strength of the passes. In Line 1, 2, and 3, you have chest passes. In Line 4, you're throwing a bounce pass, and the rebounder throws an overhead outlet to the inbound, and the inbound throws an overhead outlet back to Line 1, so it's a good mix of passing.

"In Line 3 and Line 4, you're working on V-cuts, as you're stepping into the lane to catch a pass, and the rebounder, of course, is working on jumping." Funadamentals are essential.

This drill can seem complicated at first, but following the path of the ball should simplify things. This diagram shows the early stage of the drill, when the first players begin moving. Keep your eye on the ball and you should be fine.

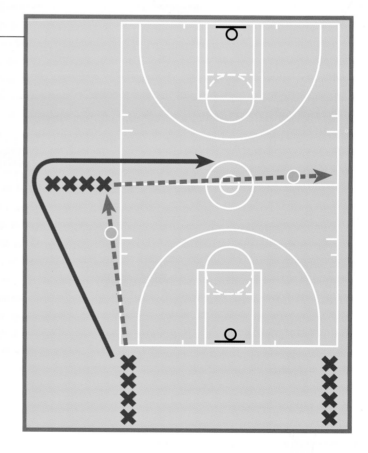

LIU

Ray Haskins is the former head coach of the Long Island University Blackbirds in Brooklyn, New York, one of America's highest-scoring teams. Charles Jones, a guard who played at LIU, led all Division I players in scoring for the 1996–97 and 1997-98 seasons.

In an effort to keep the scoreboard busy, Haskins has his players perform what he calls LIU, a three-on-two fast-break drill that features three offensive players against two defensive players.

To set up LIU, Haskins places two players on defense, one at the foul line, and a defensive partner directly behind him. A team of three offensive players is assembled to attack this two-player defensive team. At one end of the floor along the sideline, three or four players are standing in a single line. Along the other end of the floor along the sideline is another group of three or four players, also standing

in a single line. At the whistle, the three offensive players go on the attack.

"It is the job of the defender at the foul line to stop the player with the ball," says Haskins. "The second defender must run out and play the offensive player who catches the first pass. The first defender must then step down into the passing lane to protect against the next pass."

When the defenders gain possession of the ball after a miss, turnover, or made basket, the three offensive players rush off the floor, and the two defensive players turn to offense.

At the other end of the floor, two new players run onto the court – these two players will be the two new defenders. At the end of the floor closest to the action, the first player along that sideline will run onto the floor and become the third offensive player. From here, the drill continues up and down the floor.

"Often times, you see teams come down the floor with a player or two advantage, and mishandle the ball. The value of this drill is in learning how to handle a three-on-two situation," says Haskins. Doing so successfully will improve your game.

COACH'S CORNER

"THIS IS A GREAT DRILL BECAUSE YOU'RE ALSO LEARNING HOW TO DEFEND WHEN YOU'RE SHORT-HANDED, SO PLAYERS ON BOTH ENDS OF THE BALL ARE REALLY GETTING A LOT OUT OF IT."

RAY HASKINS, HEAD COACH, LONG ISLAND UNIVERSITY BLACKBIRDS, NEW YORK

THREE-MAN SHOOTING DRILL

In an effort to keep his shooters sharp, Ray Haskins often uses a Three-Man Shooting Drill, a basic catch-and-shoot drill that requires three players: a shooter, who is anywhere on the floor he feels he needs to be practicing from; a rebounder positioned beneath the basket, and a passer set up to the right or left of the shooter.

When the shooter releases his shot, the ball is rebounded – quickly "pitched" or heaved out – to the passer or "outlet," whose job it is to whip a quick pass back to the shooter and to keep the shooter's release in rhythm. This drill should be smooth as silk when performed correctly.

"We try and give each shooter ten shots before we start rotating positions," says Haskins, who runs this exercise approximately ten minutes in each practice.

"Everything we practice are things that we are going to face in game situations," says Haskins. "A guy catching and shooting, a guy rebounding and pitching to the outlet, all of that happens in every single game."

ELBOW-TO-ELBOW

odger Blind, the head basketball coach at St Peter's College in Jersey City, New Jersey, shared one of his favorite offensive drills for this project, a shooting exercise he calls Elbow-to-Elbow, or Twelve-feet-to-Twelve-feet (the width of the lane in college basketball).

For this drill, three players and two basketballs are required: a rebounder under the basket holding a ball, a shooter on one elbow – which is the right angle at the ends of the free-throw line – and a passer on the opposite wing, who is also holding a ball.

If the shooter is starting from the right elbow, the drill works as follows. At the whistle, the shooter sprints across the floor to the left elbow. He takes a pass from the passer, who is standing on the left wing, extended from the foul line. After receiving the pass, the shooter squares up to the basket, and takes a shot. As he is shooting the ball, the rebounder tosses the second ball in play to the passer, and goes to rebound the first shot.

After the shooter takes his first shot, he quickly runs back to the right elbow, where the passer zips him another pass. The player catches, squares up again, and shoots again before heading back to the left elbow, and the process continues.

"If a player can get off fifteen to eighteen shots in fifty-five seconds, that's excellent," says Blind. "In this drill, the rebounder really has to hustle. He must run down rebound after rebound and keep firing pass after pass to the passer.

"I think a big thing that kids need to understand is being ready to shoot the ball before it gets to you. Too many guys wait until they catch the ball to go into their preparation, and that's exactly what you don't want them to do."

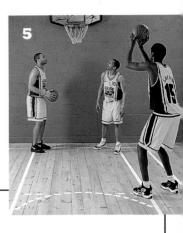

COACH'S CORNER

"IN THIS DRILL, THE SHOOTER IS LEARNING HOW TO SHOOT ON THE MOVE IN RAPID-FIRE SUCCESSION, AND SQUARING UP TO THE BASKET. THE PASSER IS WORKING ON SETTING UP THE SHOOTER BY PERFECTING HIS PASSES IN THE SHOOTING POCKET."

RODGER BLIND, HEAD COACH, ST PETER'S COLLEGE, NEW JERSEY

The player takes a shot and sets the drill in motion.

The rebound is passed quickly to the passer, positioned on the wing.

The shooter hustles the whole time to keep momentum going.

The passer must keep a ball in the shooter's hands at all times.

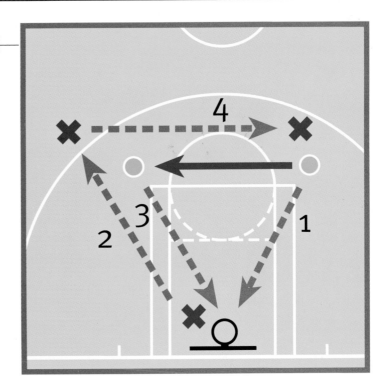

ELEVEN-MAN FAST BREAK

Wally Halas – grandson of football coach George "Papa Bear" Halas, the founder of the Chicago Bears – was the head basketball coach at Columbia University from 1987 to 1990, and Clark University from 1974 to 1987. Throughout his career, the one drill Halas enjoyed using most was the Eleven-Man Fast Break.

"This is a very good conditioning drill that works very much like a three-on-two fast break," says Halas. "One of the most important things this drill does is determine the hungriest player."

To start this drill, Halas places seven players on one end of the floor and four players on the other. Each player will be assigned a letter for this drill.

On the end of the court where seven players are standing, Halas sets up Player A at the top of the key, with Player B extended to his left and Player C extended to his right. These three players will be the attacking or offensive unit. Defending the basket will be Player D, who is positioned at the foul line, and Player E, who is standing in the 3-second area behind Player D.

Standing out of bounds on the left side of the floor – extended from the foul line – is Player F; and standing out of bounds on the right side of the floor – also extended from the foul line – is Player G.

On the other end of the floor, Player H will be standing in a defensive position at the foul line, while Player I, also on defense, will be standing behind him in the 3-second area. Standing out of bounds on the left side of the floor – extended from the foul line – is Player J, and standing out of bounds on the right side of the floor – extended from the foul line – is Player K.

At the whistle, Players A, B, and C will attack Players D and E in fast-break fashion. The offensive unit will work for one shot, and after that shot is taken (regardless of whether or not the ball goes into the basket), all five players (A through E) will fight hard for the rebound until one player emerges from the pack with the ball. During the scramble, which at times will appear more like rugby than basketball, no fouls will be called.

Let's assume that Player C emerges from the pack with the rebound. Player C will outlet, or pass the ball out, to Player G, who has just stepped onto the floor. From here, Player G will dribble the ball to the middle of the floor, and Player C (the rebounder) and Player F (the other player who had been waiting out of bounds) will now become the offensive unit. The leftover players will remain on the court with switched responsibilities. Players A and B, who had been a part of the fast break, will now take defensive positions beneath the basket where Players D and E once stood. Players D and E, originally on defense, will head out of bounds (where Players F and G stood originally) to become eventual outlet players.

As the second fast break continues, Players C, F, and G run down the other end of the floor to attack Players H and I, who are now defending the basket. As in the previous sequence, the offensive unit will get off a shot, and this time, the rebounder of that shot will join Players J and K as the next fast break unit, attacking Players A and B, who are now playing defense. From here, the drill becomes continuous, with players changing positions for each new fast break. Halas ran this drill for roughly 10–15 minutes each practice.

Halas has drawn up a list of practice-effective techniques for the three-on-three fast break:

- Safe outlet
- Ball in the middle of the floor
- Fill lanes (stay wide)
- Wings cut to the basket on a 45-degree angle
- Point guard (player who dribbled to the middle of the floor) passes to either wing (players stationed foul-line extended)
- Wing option (this includes layup) passing to opposite wing under the basket, passing back to the point guard, who sets up at the "elbow" on the same side as the wing to whom he passed
- The shot must be taken within two or three passes, maximum, or else the fast break will be over

COACH'S CORNER

"THE MAIN ELEMENTS HERE ARE LEARNING THE OUTLET PASS, BLOCKING OUT BENEATH THE BASKET, AND LEARNING TO BUILD AGGRESSIVENESS."

WALLY HALAS, FORMER HEAD BASKETBALL COACH, CLARK UNIVERSITY (1974-87) & COLUMBIA UNIVERSITY (1987-90)

SEVENTY LAYUPS IN THREE MINUTES

Glenn Braica, an assistant coach at St Francis College in Brooklyn, New York, has offered two very intense drills that the Terriers run in their daily practices. The defensive drill featured here, perhaps the toughest of all to run from a mental and physical standpoint, he calls Seventy Layups in Three Minutes. The second drill is called Terrier Transition in honor of his team, and can be found in Chapter 6.

For the Seventy Layups in Three Minutes drill, which requires 12 players, Braica will set up three lines of three players, each stretched out baseline to baseline beneath one basket, facing the opposite basket. In the middle line, the three players will be the point guards, or main ball-handlers. All three lines will be facing the opposite basket, looking as if they are about to go through the motions of a three-player weave. In the middle line, where the ball-handlers are standing, the first person will have a ball in hand. On the lines to the left and right, the second player on each of those lines, not the first, will each be holding a ball.

At the opposite end of the floor, three lines of one player each are waiting in a similar spread formation, facing the oncoming players. On these three lines, the player in the middle is without a ball, while the players to his right and left are both holding a ball.

At the whistle, the point guard holding the ball in the middle lane dribbles the ball up-court, as each of the two players from the lines on his right and left "fill the lanes" or continue on a course that flanks the point guard. When the point guard reaches the foul line, he comes to a "jump stop" at the foul line or the top of the key and makes a pass to either of the two players filling their lanes.

Whichever side the point guard passes to, the player on that side goes in for a layup. The player on the opposite side of the point guard, the wingman who did not receive the pass from the point guard, will receive a pass from the player on the one-player line directly in front of him, and take a jump shot. Meanwhile, after making the initial pass off to one of his wings, the point guard will step to the side of the floor where his initial pass traveled, and he will also receive a pass from the other player holding a ball on that side of the floor, and take a jump shot of his own.

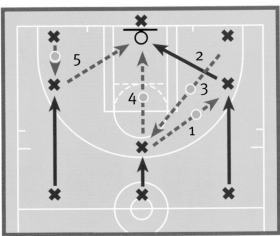

This drill is poetry in motion once in play. The point guard passes to a player in the wing (1) who goes in for a layup (2). A player near the baseline passes to the point guard (3) who takes a jump shot (4). Meanwhile, the player who did not receive a pass from the point guard receives one from a player near the baseline and also takes a jump shot.

To end this sequence, the only player who hasn't touched the ball, the player in the middle who was without a ball, steps in to rebound the initial layup, and, joined by the two players who have just played the role of passers, heads down the other end of the floor to work the same drill.

As the next team of three head down the other end of the floor, they will be greeted by three more players who will function in the roles they just performed: the player in the middle line will now be without a ball, and will end up rebounding a layup and starting another fast break. The first players on the right and left lines, who were originally holding balls as the second players in line, will now serve as passers to the oncoming team, before bolting out as wingmen on the next fast break.

"The goal here is to get off seventy shots in three minutes," says Braica. "You want to take good shots, either layups or shots from about fifteen feet out, but the seventy shots that we want must be made shots, not misses."

TWO-BALL OR PERIPHERAL PASSING DRILLS

Seton Hall Coach Tommy Amaker offers a quick-hitting ball-handling/passing drill that his Pirates often perform.

The basic Two-Ball Passing Drill or Peripheral Passing Drill that Amaker uses involves five men standing at any given spot on the floor. Four of these players (one is holding a ball) are standing in a horizontal line, two or three feet from each other. All four of these players are facing one teammate, who is standing several feet across from them, also holding a ball.

At the whistle, the player facing the group of four will quickly pass the ball to any of the three players not holding a ball on their line. Once that pass is released, the player holding the ball on the horizontal line fires a pass of his own to the initial passer. The initial passer makes the catch, passes to another open man, takes another return pass, and the passing drill just keeps picking up speed.

COACH'S CORNER

"IT'S NOT VERY INTRICATE, BUT IT'S A GOOD PASSING DRILL WE USE THAT PROVES VERY EFFECTIVE. IT HELPS GUYS HANDLE THE BALL BETTER, PASS BETTER, AND CATCH BETTER."

TOMMY AMAKER, COACH, SETON HALL

FAST BREAK NO. 1

After 30 years of coaching at North Carolina as an assistant to the great Dean Smith, Bill Guthridge took over the reins of perhaps the most elite program in the nation. Billy Cunningham, Charlie Scott, Michael Jordan, and James Worthy are just a few of the players that have rolled off the Tar Heels assembly line throughout the years.

Guthridge, who sticks to the same formula that made Smith one of the most successful coaches in the history of sports, likes his players to warm up with a familiar fast-break routine known around Chapel Hill as Fast Break No. 1.

To set up this drill, Guthridge forms three lines of four players each across the baseline, with all three lines facing the opposite basket. At the whistle, the first player on the right line will whip a pass into the hands of the first player in the middle line, who is usually the point guard.

From here, all three players will begin to run in their respective lanes toward the basket they are facing. Once the middle player catches his pass, he zips a pass around mid-court back to the initial passer from the right line. As all three players continue to run toward the basket, the player from the left line, who has not yet received a pass, will race to the extended foul-line area of the opposite basket and then make a cut toward that basket. As he cuts, the player on the right line passes him the ball for a layup.

After the shot is made, the player from the middle line will sprint to the left side of the floor, extended from the foul line. The player from the right line who made the last pass to the cutter will rebound the basketball. The player from the left line who took the shot will swing around the baseline and head back up the right side of the floor.

"This is really a loosening-up exercise," said Guthridge. "The guys really get enthused and start talking it up, and that sets a real good tone for practice."

Once all three players have assumed their new positions in transition, another fast break will begin heading down the opposite end of the floor: the rebounder will pitch out to the point guard extended at the foul line, and two more passes will be made before the next layup attempt.

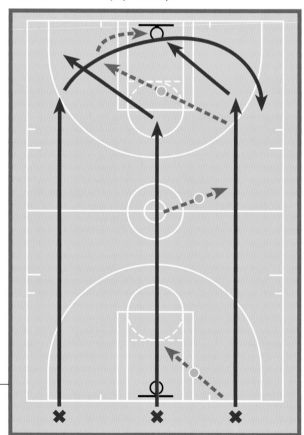

Pass and go is the name of the game in this drill, keeping the ball moving as players run down-court before cutting to the basket for a layup.

Dee-Fense

I T HAS BEEN SAID THAT DEFENSE HAS LITTLE TO DO WITH TALENT AND MORE TO DO WITH GRIT, DETERMINATION, HUSTLE AND PRIDE. EVERYONE, NO MATTER HOW TALL OR SMALL, HAS THE POTENTIAL TO BE A GREAT DEFENDER, BUT NOT MANY HAVE THE INNER QUALITIES REQUIRED TO REACH SUCH STATUS. WHILE OFFENSE SELLS TICKETS, DEFENSE USUALLY WINS BALL GAMES, WHICH IS WHY COACHES ARE ALWAYS PREACHING DEFENSE TO THEIR PLAYERS. SEVERAL OF THESE COACHES, INCLUDING HALL-OF-FAMER LENNY WILKENS, TOOK THE TIME TO PREACH IN DEFENSE OF DEFENSE, SHARING SOME OF THEIR FAVORITE DEFENSIVE STRATEGIES.

DENIAL DRILL

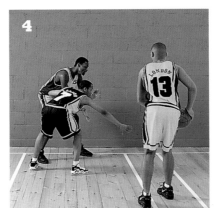

Jim Harter, the head basketball coach at Pace University in New York City, is a product of rich basketball bloodlines. Jim's father, Dick Harter, is an assistant coach with the Indiana Pacers of the National Basketball Association.

One drill which the younger Harter often uses in his practices is called the Denial Drill, a three-player defensive exercise which focuses on preventing an easy pass anywhere on the floor.

"What I'm trying to accomplish is to get our guys to extend out and make it really difficult for the pass to get through," says Harter. "This drill allows our team to aggressively deny the basketball." To set up this drill, Harter uses two offensive players and one defensive player. At the top of the key, or anywhere above the foul line, Harter places one offense player with the basketball playing the role of point guard. A second offensive player sets up on the right or left wing, and the lone defender is out on the same wing, attempting to "deny" the pass to the intended receiver by taking two steps off the receiver toward the ball, and one step in the passing lane.

"It doesn't matter where the offensive and defensive players are positioned on the floor," says Harter. "The key is for the defensive player to overplay the offensive player, not allowing the offensive player to catch the ball in a desired spot on the floor."

RUN-GLIDE-RUN

Jerry "The Shark" Tarkanian, who currently coaches at Fresno State University in California, was a legendary coach at the University of Nevada, Las Vegas, where he won a championship in 1990. Over the years, Tarkanian has produced a number of quality NBA players like Reggie Theus, Sidney Green, and Larry Johnson.

One drill that Tarkanian loves to use in his practices is called Run-Glide-Run. To set up this drill, Coach Tarkanian places the ball-handler on either the right or left wing of the court, extended from the foul line. If the play is set up on the right side of the floor, the ball-handler, at the sound of the whistle, will take the first step heading toward the baseline.

Beaten by a step, the defender will turn and place his shoulders perpendicular to the dribbler's direction – in this case the baseline. The defender will then point his foot in the direction he is heading – "rather than step and slide, like most people do," says Tarkanian – and then get really low to the point where the defender's chest is on his knee.

From here, the defender will take as long a stride as possible toward the ball-handler without ever looking at the ball-handler. (Since this play is developing on the right side of the floor, the defender will be taking that first long stride with his right foot.) The defender should then take another long stride with his left foot "and that should cover the ground that was lost."

Once the lost ground has been made up, the defender should pivot and lock the dribbler back in a low, wide stance.

"When a defender gets beat, he usually tries to just slide along with the dribbler and hope that the help comes over to trap him," says Tarkanian. "The goal here is to take one or two long strides and make up that lost ground, and to get back in front of the ball-handler."

And of course, Tarkanian's playbook is equipped with the long version of Run-Glide-Run.

"If your man really has you beat, you do the same steps, but not only do you take a first long step, but a second long step and a third long step and then you lock the dribbler in," he says. "The long version of this drill is normally used when you're pressing in a full-court situation.

"But either way, you must first start to practice this drill slowly, even without a ball," says Tarkanian. "The main idea is to get technique down." Learn the technique and make these moves second nature.

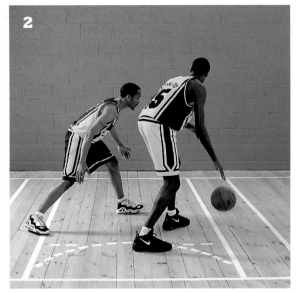

COACH'S CORNER

"THE PURPOSE OF THIS DRILL IS FOR THE MAN GUARDING THE DRIBBLER TO COVER GROUND WHEN HE HAS BEEN BEATEN BY THE DRIBBLER. RATHER THAN JUST WAIT FOR YOUR HELP, THIS DRILL WILL HELP YOU RECOVER QUICKLY BY YOURSELF."

JERRY TARKANIAN, COACH, FRESNO STATE UNIVERSITY, CALIFORNIA

HAND ON THE BALL

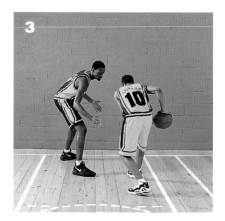

Manhattan College Men's Coach John Leonard has contributed four drills (Hand On The Ball, Straight Denial, Deny The Flash, and Four-On-Two) covering some of the vitals of defensive play.

For this first drill, three players are needed: an offensive player, a defensive player, and a substitute. The offensive player stands foul-line extended with the ball. The defensive player guarding the ball is also foul-line extended.

The player with the ball jabs (or moves his non-pivot foot) in several different directions as if he is going to make a move toward the basket, jabbing his foot out some six to eight inches, but does not dribble. The defender must react to those jabs, taking half a step back each time. The offensive player keeps the ball in the triple-threat position, which is at his hip.

After the defensive player reacts to several jabs, the offensive player rocks back as if to release a pass, and now the defensive player must learn how to hop, taking his momentum half a step back up toward the offensive player, to pressure the basketball.

After six or seven seconds, Coach Leonard yells "Play live" and the two players will play each other one-on-one. When playing live, the offensive player is limited to just two dribbles, which teaches the player how to beat the defender off a quick-foot fake or a shot-fake. At the same time, the defensive player learns how to guard a player who has not used his dribble yet. When that dribble is finally used, the defensive player's primary goal is to head off the dribbler toward the sideline. The defender also learns how to contest a shot, box out, and finally, to retrieve the basketball. When the coach blows the whistle, the defensive player walks off, the offensive player switches to defense, and the substitute goes in to plays offense.

"This is an extremely quick drill, designed for just a couple of minutes," says Leonard. "In a few minutes, each guy should get two or three repetitions. Also, the good thing about this drill, and many of our other drills, is that it allows a player to sharpen his skills on offense as well as defense."

STRAIGHT DENIAL

Select three players. One player holding the basketball goes to the middle of the floor in the area at the top of the key. One offensive player and one defensive player are placed at the wing position, the area on either side of the floor extended from the foul line.

"The purpose of this drill is to teach the defensive player how to deny a penetration pass, or a pass that goes forward toward the basket," says Leonard. In order to accomplish this, he places his defensive player two steps off the offensive player toward the ball, and one step in the passing lane. As the player holding the ball attempts to pass it into the offensive player, the offensive player is learning how to use various cuts to the basket to free himself from the defender.

In the meantime, the defensive player is learning how to deny a penetration pass, and adjust his positioning to counterattack the moves of the offensive player, who is working hard to get free. If the offensive player slips by the defensive player, and catches the pass, Coach Leonard will let his players play "live, one-on-one" again in order to finish the play. In the meantime, the player passing the ball is practicing the art of finding a receiver who is on the move.

DENY THE FLASH

Gather six players. Place a player with the ball on the right wing. Place a defensive player in the "help position," in the middle of the lane. Line up four players on the baseline of the "weakside," the side of the floor without the ball.

The player covering defense is going to guard all four of the players waiting on the weakside. He will be in a position where he is pointing to the ball and to the player he will be guarding. The first player from the weakside flashes to the foul line.

"As soon as he starts to flash and gets into the lane area, we have to make body contact with him," says Leonard. "The defensive player wants to deny the offensive player the 'flash' or burst up the lane." When the offensive player gets near the foul line, he tries to back-cut to the basket.

From this point, the defensive player must put his chest into the body of the offensive player trying to make his way up the lane toward the rim. The defensive player must continue to prevent the flashing player from driving down the lane toward the hoop. Once the defender has driven off the flasher, the next player waiting on the weakside flashes to the foul line, and the drill continues as before, with variations of offensive moves and defensive countermoves to follow. The player who first flashed to the foul line becomes the next defensive player after one rotation.

FOUR-ON-TWO

COACH'S CORNER

"WE THINK VERY HIGHLY OF THESE DRILLS BECAUSE THEY ARE A GREAT TEACHING DEVICE FOR COVERING A LOT OF CONCEPTS ON DEFENSE, AND ON THE FLIP SIDE, YOU'RE ALSO WORKING ON OFFENSE."

JOHN LEONARD, HEAD COACH, MANHATTAN COLLEGE

Gather six players. Place four players on offense, two forwards and two guards. The other two players are on defense. The guards are in their normal position and the forwards are in the corners of the court, as if they are in a box set. For the purpose of this drill, the ball is allowed to move only from one guard to the other.

One of the guards takes the ball, and the two players on defense are now playing against all four offensive players. The two defenders, however, guard the forwards.

Whichever forward is on the side of the ball, the defender must deny the potential "penetration pass," falling back on the Straight Denial drill. The second defender is now in the middle of the lane, in the help position, defending against the possibility of the second forward flashing up to the foul line as the earlier drill. Since the offense is allowed to pass the ball guard-to-guard, as soon as the ball is airborne, the defensive player who was in the help position must learn to sprint out and deny the corner man on the ball. At the same time, the defender who was denying the initial forward in the corner must now learn how to sprint while the ball is in flight to the "help position."

"This last drill is the toughest," says Leonard. "At any time, the coach can yell 'shot!' One of the two guards will shoot the ball, and now the two guards who were playing defense must learn to box out the guys in the corner.

"We run all four of these drills each and every practice," says Leonard. "Combined, they should take a total of about eight to ten minutes." A short drill, it keeps players in real play mode.

FOUR-ON-THREE OVERLOAD

Rodger Blind, who contributed an offensive drill called Elbow to Elbow for Chapter 4, offers this defensive drill from the playbook of former New York Knicks coach Hubie Brown – the Four-on-Three Overload drill. The objective of this drill is to teach his players how to play fast-break defense.

Here is the way Blind sets up his Four-on-Three Overload: Four players wearing white shirts are placed out of bounds on the baseline facing the opposite basket. Four players wearing blue shirts are placed on the foul line, spread across the width of the court facing the whites.

The coach, holding the basketball, stands in the middle of the blue shirts. The coach rolls the ball to any one of the four white shirts on the baseline. As soon as one of those players touches the ball, all four of the white shirts must immediately fast-break toward the other end of the court.

Meanwhile, the blue shirts, who are at the foul line with about a 15-foot lead, wait for the coach to yell out the name or number of a player from their line. When the coach yells out a player's name or number, that player must run and sprint to the baseline and touch it. While the player called is touching the baseline, the other three blue shirts immediately sprint back, setting up a four-on-three fast-break with defensive help – in the form of the blue shirt who ran back to touch the baseline – on the way.

"From there, if you let the kids play, what you work on is having one of the blue shirts, or one of the

defenders, stopping the basketball," says Blind. "Kids right away think, 'I have to try and steal the ball from the dribbler,' but you don't want to do that: you want to slow the dribbler down."

By teaching players to slow down the dribbler, Blind is forcing the dribbler toward one of the sidelines rather than letting the dribbling go in a straight line toward the basket.

At any time, a player on the white team can pass the ball to one of his teammates, so one of the two defenders must sprint back and anticipate the next pass, leaving his defensive partner guessing as to which offensive player he will shadow.

"Depending on the situation, the player must know if he is guarding the ball or guarding the player without the ball," says Blind. "It's a really good drill because there are so many things that can happen."

For this drill, Coach Blind uses a four-on-four setup because "it makes the court bigger in terms of the players being spread out," he says. "It also makes it a lot harder on the defense in terms of what they should do, when they should do it, and, in the end, why they should do it. The eventual goal is to buy time for that fourth defender to get back and even up the numbers."

At the beginning of this drill, players wait in anticipation on the baseline and foul-line for the signal before setting up the four-on-three play that is at its heart.

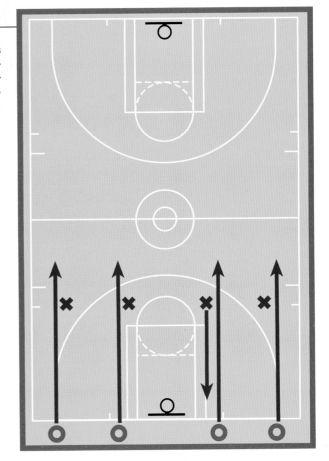

COACH'S CORNER

"ONE THING YOU REALLY HAVE TO STRESS TO KIDS IS THAT IN THE FAST BREAK, YOU MAY HAVE TO COVER A MAN THAT IS NOT NECESSARILY YOURS. FOR EXAMPLE, A GUARD MAY BE PLAYING A BIG MAN OR A BIG MAN MAY BE PLAYING A GUARD."

RODGER BLIND, HEAD COACH, ST PETER'S COLLEGE, NEW JERSEY

FOUR-ON-FOUR SHELL DEFENSE

Jack Armstrong is the head coach at Niagara University in western New York, and his Purple Eagles play in the tough Metro Atlantic Athletic Conference. For this project, Armstrong shares his favorite defensive drill, one which he calls Four-on-Four Shell Defense.

"With this drill, you are basically teaching team defense," says Armstrong. "Mainly, what you are trying to concentrate on is ball-side defense and help-side defense."

In setting up this drill, Armstrong places a piece of tape down the center of the lane. The coach then places two players on each side of the tape, or each side of the court. On the right side of the court, one player is holding the ball on a wing, and a second player is standing in the corner. A third player is set up on the opposite wing, and a fourth player is set up in the opposite corner. Four defenders are inserted to guard these players at each of their respective positions.

"What you want to do now is work with the one defender who is guarding the player with the ball, how he is playing the ball," says Armstrong. "And then you want to concentrate on the player who is guarding the player one pass away on the same side of the floor – which is called ball side."

On the left side of the floor, or across the piece of tape – this is where the help-side defense is located – Armstrong has a third defensive player, the one guarding the offensive player on the wing, in a help position or what is known in coaching circles as a "Ball-You-Man" position.

"In this position, the defender can see the ball as he is just one pass away, and he can also see his own man, so he is in a position to help," says Armstrong. "And then the player guarding the player in the opposite left-hand corner is two passes away.

"The tape we put down right in the middle of the lane separates the ball-side defense from the weakside defense," Armstrong added. "If the guy is on the right side, you're on the ball side, if you're on the left side, you're in help side.

"Now we want the guys who are in help side to be on that line, so that if the ball is driven to the basket they will be in a position to help."

Another simple drill that Armstrong uses for his struggling shooters is letting them work one-on-one with a toss-back machine. This device allows a player to throw the ball against it, and will return the ball to the player as if a teammate on the floor were tossing him a pass.

By receiving constant passes from the toss-back machine, a player can spend long hours in the gym concentrating solely on his shot.

"This exercise is great because the ball is coming back to you at game-like speed," says Armstrong. "One catch though, you have to try and talk the team manager or your girlfriend into rebounding for you."

HAWKS THREE-ON-THREE DEFENSIVE DRILL

Who better to offer a hoop drill than the winningest coach in NBA history? Lenny Wilkens, once a star player in the NBA, has seen his star shine even brighter since his playing days came to an end.

Entering the 1997–98 season, his 25th season as an NBA head coach, Wilkens had compiled a career record of 1,070 victories – the most coaching victories in the history of the sport – against 876 losses with Seattle, Portland, Cleveland, and Atlanta. As coach of the Seattle SuperSonics in the 1977–78 season, Wilkens won his only NBA championship.

For this project, Coach Wilkens shared a drill he calls the Hawks Three-on-Three Defensive Drill – "one of my favorites."

To set up this drill, Wilkens uses six players, three on offense and three on defense. One offensive player is set up behind the end line beneath the basket, in a position to inbound the basketball. A second offensive player is on one side of the floor, extended from the foul line, or "on the wing." A third offensive player is on the opposite side of the floor, also out on a wing.

The defensive setup includes one long-armed defender guarding the player who will attempt to inbound the ball. Each of the other two defenders is guarding the offensive players out on their respective wings.

"What I'm trying to teach in this drill is pressing and double-teaming," says Wilkens. "What we do in this drill is try to force the ball to the side of the floor that we want it on, and then force a trap."

In order to pull off this defensive strategy, Wilkens will maneuver his defenders accordingly. If Wilkens would like to see the offense work from the right side of the floor, he will allow the defender guarding the inbounder to take a step back, at the same time asking that defender to turn his back in the direction of the offensive player on the left side of the floor, tempting the inbounder to look at the right side of the floor. At the same time, Wilkens will take the defender guarding the offensive player on the right wing and also allow him to take a step back off of his player. Meanwhile, the defender on the left wing will tighten the defense on his player. If all three defensive players are doing their jobs properly, the inbounder should instinctively opt to pass the ball to the right side of the floor. Remember, the inbounder has only five seconds in which to inbound the ball to a teammate.

"The reason we want to influence the ball is to get it into the hands of the weaker of the two ball-handlers on offense," says Wilkens. "Then we drop back to zone the area, and pick our spot to trap."

Once the ball is inbounded on the right side of the floor, the defensive player on that side immediately closes in on his player. At the same time, the defender who was guarding the inbounder rushes to help the right-wing defender, and the two attempt to surround the offensive player, or trap him, hoping to force a turnover. Once the trap is in progress, the defender from the left-wing position will, as Wilkens described, "zone the area," hoping to intercept a hurried pass thrown by the trapped offensive player to one of his open teammates.

Also remember: once the ball is inbounded, the offensive unit then has just 10 seconds to get the ball over the half-court line.

"Part of this drill requires our offensive players to dribble the ball over the half-court line, and not pass it over," says Wilkens. "That's part of the drill to get us used to trapping and double-teaming." According to Wilkens, the offense is also benefitting.

"If we know the person receiving the inbounds pass is being guarded by a weak defender, we tell him to push the ball hard, and do not allow the trap to happen," says Wilkens. "Or, if the player does get trapped, then he must pass the ball back to the inbound, whose job it will be to push it up the floor. This makes it important to have a good ball-handler inbounding the ball."

THREE-UP, TWO-DOWN

R on St John, a former player at York College in Jamaica, New York, in the 1970s, has been the head coach of his old team for more than a decade. In 1997, St John led York to a City University of New York Division III championship.

One of the drills that St John enjoys most is a fast-break, defensive exercise he calls Three-Up, Two-Down.

To set up this drill, St John sets up three offensive lines of two or three players each at one end of the court facing the opposite basket, and two defenders waiting for them at the other end of the court. At the whistle, the first player in the middle of the three offensive lines, acting as a

point guard, will dribble the ball toward the two defenders, with his offensive partners serving as wing men on the fast break.

As they approach the two defenders, the three offensive players will try to find the open player, and take a shot. Once that shot is taken, the offensive player in the middle of the floor will quickly switch back to defense, and the two players who were playing defense in the original sequence will switch to offense, and those two players will now start their own two-on-one fast break in the other direction.

"You only get one shot at the basket, and are not allowed to fight for an offensive rebound,"

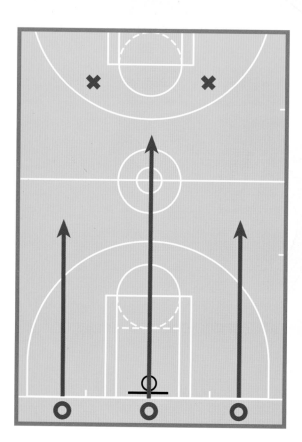

JUMP SWITCH
ON SWITCHING, OR SWAPPING OF PLAYERS BEING GUARDED, A MOVE INTO THE PATH OF THE DRIBBLER TO FORCE THE PLAYER EITHER TO THE BASELINE OR STOP THE ADVANCE OF THE BALL.

says St John, who rotates players at each end of the floor to keep the drill in constant motion. "Whether you make it or not doesn't matter: the idea is to learn how to do the little things on the fast break, like the point guard stopping at the foul line to take a jumper or making a pass to a wing man who will cut in for a layup. And then we're concentrating on transition, where the defense grabs the ball and goes on an offensive attack.

"I like this drill because all of us know that players can execute a three-on-one fast break with no problem, but when you get your players to execute a three-on-two fast break, that means you have a lot of teamwork involved," says St John.

Once the second basket is or isn't made, three new players from the original side of the floor will spring into action against the two defenders who are waiting to guard against the fast break. These two defenders will be the players who performed as the original wing men on the first fast break.

"This is all about transition and learning how to play defense," says St John, who runs this drill for seven to ten minutes per practice. "It's nonstop running and nonstop thinking."

ZIGZAG

Another defensive drill that Ron St John favors greatly is called the Zigzag. St John had always used this drill and became even more of a believer in it when the Duke coach Mike Krzyzewski, who pilots one of the elite basketball programs in America, spoke so highly of it at a basketball clinic that St John attended.

To set up this drill, St John sets up one line of offensive players beginning at the corner of the baseline on one end of the floor. Looking up-court, St John draws up a tight boundary between the sideline on the player's right and an imaginary line parallel to the nearest line that runs along the foul lane to the player's left. At the whistle, the job of the offensive player will be to dribble the ball in V-like formations from sideline to imaginary line. The offensive player must keep his zigzag dribble alive in his tight boundary despite the presence of a defensive player who is trying to steal the ball or disrupt his dribble. The defensive player is learning the proper way to slide his feet, which is extremely important in keeping his balance, and not letting the offensive player speed past him or force him to commit a bad foul.

"The idea of this drill is for the offensive player to work on his dribbling in the presence of a defender," says St John. "As for the defense, we expect him to move his legs by sliding and not to turn sideways. If the defensive player can learn to beat the offensive player to a certain spot on the floor and keep his body square to the offensive, he will end up drawing a lot of offensive fouls."

After his defenders get comfortable with guarding the zigzagging dribblers, St John has them play defense all over again, but this time, they must keep their hands behind their backs.

"When you're playing a guy, he doesn't run straight at you because he'll run you over. He goes lateral," says St John. "So what you have to do is beat him to that spot and get right in front of him - slide, slide, slide."

4

COACH'S CORNER

"A LOT OF DEFENDERS WANT TO PLAY
DEFENSE USING THEIR HANDS, BUT THIS DRILL
IS ALL ABOUT LEGS AND LATERAL
MOVEMENT."

RON ST JOHN, HEAD COACH, YORK COLLEGE, NEW YORK

Transition Drills

TRANSITION DRILLS ARE THE MOST COMPREHENSIVE, MOST CHALLENGING, MOST EXHAUSTING HOOP DRILLS OF ALL. PLAYERS ENDURE UP-AND-DOWN, BACK-AND-FORTH, OFFENSE-TO-DEFENSE AND DEFENSE-TO-OFFENSE PLAY THAT CATCHES AN OPPONENT OFF-GUARD BY SCORING EASY BASKETS. TRANSITION BASKETBALL ALSO CONFUSES OPPONENTS WITH ALERT "GET BACK" DEFENSE, AND CAN SIMPLY WEAR OUT AN OPPONENT FROM A PHYSICAL STANDPOINT. THE BEST TRANSITION TEAMS ARE USUALLY THOSE WITH THE BEST-CONDITIONED ATHLETES AND THE HARDEST WORKERS. A TEAM WHICH EXCELS IN TRANSITION CAN OFTEN OFFSET AN OPPONENT'S ADVANTAGE IN SIZE OR OVERALL TALENT BY KEEPING THAT OPPONENT ON THE RUN AND OUT OF ITS DESIRED SET ATTACK ON OFFENSE AND DEFENSE.

CIRCLE REBOUND

J ay Wright, the head basketball coach at Hofstra University on Long Island, New York, has contributed two unique drills to this book: a team exercise called the Circle Rebound drill; and an individual exercise, Repeats (see Chapter 4).

As Coach Wright explains, Circle Rebound is a five-on-five team drill that emphasizes the aggressiveness of pursuing the basketball, rebounding, and transition offense and defense.

"A lot of people feel the key to rebounding is boxing out," says Wright. "But the real key to rebounding is going after the ball."

Here is how the Circle Rebound Drill works: One coach stands at the foul line holding the basketball. Ten players form a circle around him. In alternating positions, five players are wearing blue jerseys, five players are wearing gold jerseys so that they are blue-gold-blue-gold all the way around the circle. At the whistle, all the players begin jogging in a circle around the coach, just as if they were playing musical chairs. The coach then throws the ball off the backboard, and all 10 players scramble for the rebound as if in a real game. Whoever gets the ball, blue or gold, becomes the offensive team.

It is now the offensive team's job to try to run out on a conventional fast break, a three-on-two or two-on-one player advantage. The team that doesn't get the ball must sprint back and convert on defense. This is a great drill to keep players on the ball both mentally and physically.

"In the initial part of this drill, we see who's tough and who is going after the ball," says Wright. "In the second part of this drill, the goal is for the offensive team to get down on a fast break and the defense has to get back in time to stop them."

THE CHANGE

Steve Lappas, the head coach at Villanova University in Pennsylvania, coaches some of the top college prospects in the nation. Kerry Kittles of the New Jersey Nets and Tim Thomas of the Philadelphia 76ers are two of Lappas's former pupils who are now earning a living in the National Basketball Association.

For this book, Lappas has contributed two of his favorite drills. The first drill is called The Change. This dribbling drill, simple to explain, is absolute murder on the basketball court.

At the whistle, five players begin dribbling the ball in a half-court set, where they are defended by five other players. Play continues until the second whistle, which means that the offensive and defensive units must change position on the floor.

When the two units switch, no two players who were guarding each other in the previous offensive set are allowed to guard each other again, which leads to initial craziness on the floor, but settles into a well-disciplined exercise.

"This way, my players are learning how to scramble, how to talk, and how to communicate out there on the floor," says Lappas. "It's also good in learning transition defense and offense."

In the middle of this drill, Lappas will add a wrinkle. At any time, the coach will yell "five on four," which tells the defense that one of its players must quickly rush off the floor. In this case, the four defenders must scramble to guard the offensive players.

"Now, the defensive players must look around and quickly see who is the least vulnerable guy on the floor," says Lappas. "They must make proper decisions quickly, and make them on the fly, and, of course, on their own." Lappas usually runs this transition drill for five to seven minutes in each of his practices.

COACH'S CORNER

"COMMUNICATION IS SO IMPORTANT IN BASKETBALL. THAT'S WHY THIS DRILL IS SO IMPORTANT."

STEVE LAPPAS, HEAD COACH, VILLANOVA UNIVERSITY, PENNSYLVANIA

NUMBER TRANSITION

S teve Lappas calls his second drill the Number Transition, which is basically a defensive transition drill. In this exercise, five players are lined up across the foul line, and five additional players are lined up at the baseline on the same side of the floor.

The team that is lined up on the foul line is the defensive team and the team lined up on the baseline is the offensive team. Every member of the defensive team is issued a number from one through five. Lappas will then shout out two numbers, and, at the same time, throw the ball to the team on the baseline. The team on the baseline will run a fast break, meaning they will have a numbers advantage heading toward the basket. The two numbers that Lappas called, which are from the defensive unit, must burst from the foul line, run and touch the baseline, race to catch up to the offensive team which is running the fast break, and eventually help out their three defensive partners who are attempting to hold the fort until they get back into the action.

"Here, once again, we are learning how to run back in transition and locate people," says Lappas. "You are starting out with just three defensive players guarding five other players, and now those other guys come into the picture, and everyone has to communicate with each other."

FOUR-ON-FIVE, FIVE-ON-FOUR, FOUR-ON-FIVE

George Karl, the former head coach of the Seattle SuperSonics, has had his talented club in the championship hunt for nearly a decade. Year after year, the Sonics are one of the most competitive teams in the National Basketball Conference.

Karl, who brushed up on his Xs and Os in the Continental Basketball Association before making his leap to the NBA, shared one drill for this project that he often runs with dynamic players like All-Stars Gary Payton and Vin Baker.

"My favorite drill is called the Four-on-Five, Five-on-Four, Four-on-Five drill," says Karl. "It's a great drill that works both offense and defense."

To set up this drill, Karl places nine players on one end of the court. Five of those players will play defense against four attacking offensive players. The exact positioning of the defensive players will be dictated by the positions that the offense players take up on the floor.

At the whistle, Karl has his five defensive players use their one-player advantage to place intense defensive pressure on the four offensive players, trapping them, double-teaming them or doing whatever it takes to try to force the offensive unit into a missed shot or a turnover.

If a shot is missed, the defensive unit will rebound the basketball, and become the offensive team in transition. This time, the offensive unit will have the one-player advantage, and the main objective on offense will be to sprint down to the other end of the floor on a five-on-four fast break and attempt to score a basket within seven

seconds of the initial rebound. After a basket is made, Karl will instruct his five offensive players to "go full-court, man-to-man pickup," in an attempt to prevent the transition offense from getting to mid-court. As in the opening sequence, the defensive team now has the advantage and will try to force the offense into a turnover.

"Five-on-four scoring in seven seconds is hard when you have to go the full length of the court in that time," says Karl. "It's a difficult thing to rebound, run the floor, find the open player and then score all in seven seconds. This is basically a pressure-defensive drill." The more pressure, the more prepared the players.

TERRIER TRANSITION & FAST BREAK

Glenn Braica, who also contributed the Seventy Layups in Three Minutes drill in Chapter 4, offers these intense drills in honor of his St Francis College team, the Terriers. In the Terrier Transition drill, which requires 10 players at one time, five players are spread across the foul line, from sideline to sideline, facing the baseline. Five other players are spread out across the baseline, each player facing an opposing player.

"What we want here is five players matching up against five other players," says Braica. "The five players on the baseline will become the offensive unit, and they will run the fast break against four of the players along the foul line, who will run back and play defense."

At the whistle, a player holding the ball at the foul line, or a coach standing out of bounds, will pass the ball to any one of the five players spread out along the baseline. That player will take the ball inbounds and, with his four teammates, begin a fast break. In order to give the offensive unit a five-on-four advantage, the player along the foul line who was standing directly across from the player who received the initial pass must race ahead to touch the baseline against the flow of the offense (similar to Steve Lappas's Number Transition drill earlier in the chapter). While that player is running toward the baseline, the five-on-four is developing. After touching the baseline, the fifth defensive player will race back to his team and even up the numbers.

"This is a great way to practice running the fast break," says Braica. "The players on offense and defense are learning how to make good decisions."

Another version of the Terrier transition play is the Terrier Fast Break, a drill that St Francis uses which involves five offensive players running the floor against three or four imaginary defenders. The purpose of this exercise is to prepare players running the fast break to be in the best possible scoring position just before releasing their shots.

To set up this exercise, five offensive players start on one end of the floor. The point guard will start at the foul line. The two tallest players will take up positions in the lane, and the two other players will start from the opposite corners of the baseline.

At the whistle, a coach will make a layup, and the tallest player on the floor, usually the center, will rebound. The rebounder, now standing behind the baseline, will outlet the ball to the point guard, who is between the foul line and the sideline. It is imperative that the point guard catch the pass with his back facing the right sideline in order to see the defense cleanly. From here, the fast break begins, as all five players run their respective lanes. The two

---

COACH'S CORNER

"THIS IS A TOUGH DRILL THAT ALSO BUILDS STAMINA AND BALL HANDLING WHEN THE PLAYERS ARE TIRED."

GLENN BRACIA, ASSISTANT COACH, ST FRANCIS COLLEGE, NEW YORK

players who started at the opposite corners are running the right and left sides of the floor. The first big player to break from the back is following the point guard, and takes a post-up position at the low block on the side of the court that the point guard has dribbled to. This will be the only player who will take a layup. The tallest player, the one who rebounded the initial layup, trails the play, and sets up along the foul line or top of the key for a jumper.

On the first trip down the floor, one player will get off a shot, and during the course of the drill every player running his lane will get to take a shot from his respective position.

"Let's say that one of the wings takes a pass from the point guard and gets off a shot," says Braica. "Now we get the rebound and go the other way to set up the next shooter, until all five guys have made a shot. All five shots must be made within a minute."

Dennis O'Donnell, the head coach at St. Thomas Aquinas College in Sparkill, New York, has built one of the top Division II programs in the United States. For this project, O'Donnell has shared a fun two-way drill he calls Battle Fatigue. To set up this drill, O'Donnell works in a half-court set, usually pitting three offensive players against three defensive players in what appears to be a regular pickup game.

"We start off three-on-three at the beginning of every year, and then we build it up to four-on-four and then five-on-five," says O'Donnell. "Every once in a while, we'll give an advantage to the offense.

"Instead of the kids playing three-on-three, I'll throw in some different restrictions," says O'Donnell. "I'll tell the team on offense that they are allowed just one dribble, or maybe two dribbles, or maybe no dribble at all before taking a shot at the basket." If, for example, the offensive team is allowed to take only one dribble, then the player who is holding the ball after that dribble is made must either shoot the ball or pass it off to a teammate. If a pass is made, then the receiving player has the same two options, pass or shoot, but does not have the luxury of dribbling.

"Basically, what you're doing is, instead of telling the kids 'Pass, pass, pass' and waiting for a good look at the basket, you're telling the kid, 'As soon as you get a good look at the basket, shoot the ball,'" he says. O'Donnell, who usually makes this game a part of every one of his practices, will award a victory to the team that scores the most baskets. If the offensive unit misses on a shot attempt, it will switch to defense, and the

defensive team that held will go on offense. This is the heart of a transition drill, the change-over.

"The best time to play this game is when the guys are exhausted," says O'Donnell. "In a real game players will be shooting when they're tired, and this is kind of why we call this drill Battle Fatigue. From a defensive perspective, we really are battling it out.

"Defensively, you're training to get up and put pressure on the ball as soon as someone catches it," O'Donnell adds. "We know that everyone likes to shoot the basketball, but one of the things that we try to sell our guys on is that in order for us to be successful, we've got to be a really good defensive team.

"In many situations, instead of the defense dictating to the offense as to what they can do, the defense is waiting for the offense to do something and then reacting to it," he says. "Here, when the offensive player catches the basketball, the defense wants to dictate to the offensive player where he can go on the floor, and whether or not he'll be able to shoot the ball. If the offensive player can get a shot off, then the defensive player is not doing his job."

Battle Fatigue really comes into play when O'Donnell places more offensive players than defensive players on the court.

"I'll put six offensive players on four defensive players and tell the offense that they are allowed as many passes as they'd like," says O'Donnell. "When I do that, the offensive guys will put big grins on their faces because they know that they're going to make twenty-five passes, drive the four defenders into the ground because they're so tired, and then they'll just drive the lane and make a layup."

COACH'S CORNER

"KIDS ENJOY THIS TYPE OF EXERCISE MORE BECAUSE IN A REGULAR DRILL, THERE IS NO WINNER OR LOSER. THIS WAY, EACH PLAYER HAS A FEELING OF PLAYING WITH TWO TEAMMATES, AND THE GOAL IS TO EITHER SCORE A BASKET OR PREVENT ONE."

DENNIS O'DONNELL, HEAD COACH, ST THOMAS AQUINAS COLLEGE, NEW YORK

THREE-ON-TWO CONDITIONER

John Wooden, the legendary UCLA coach who guided the Bruins to a record ten National Collegiate Athletic Association championships from 1948 to 1975 (including seven consecutive championships from 1966 to 1973) as well as an unprecedented 88-game winning streak from the 1970–71 season to the 1973–74 campaign, and worked with the basketball greats Kareem Abdul-Jabaar, Bill Walton, and Marques Johnson, had a ten-minute drill he would incorporate into every practice, the Three-on-Two Conditioner. The purpose of this drill is to teach an offense how to run a three-on-two fast break, and to teach a defense the proper way to defend against it. In setting up the Three-on-Two Conditioner, Wooden liked to use an odd number of players, preferably 11 or 13.

Using 13 players, the drill is set up by placing three players underneath one backboard. One group of five players is standing just beyond mid-court, out of bounds, on the right side of the floor. A second group of five players is just beyond mid-court, out of bounds, on the left side of the floor.

At the whistle, both the offense and the defense start moving. One of the three players beneath the basket tosses himself a pass off the backboard, and all three players, now on offense, turn and steam down the other end of the floor in an attempt to score a basket.

As soon as the first player gives himself a pass off the backboard, the first player in one group of five (the side of the floor is determined by the coach) races out to the bottom of the half-court circle, touches the hardwood, and sprints back to a defensive position within the 3-second area of the lane. As soon as the first defensive player touches the half-court circle, a second player from the group of five races out to mid-court, touches the bottom of the circle, and heads back into a defensive position between the foul line and the top of the half-court circle.

As soon as the three offensive players cross mid-court, a third defensive player comes off the sideline, touches the bottom of the mid-court circle and races past the offense and into a defensive position on the floor to help out his defensive partners, who are momentarily outnumbered.

"It's constant motion," says Wooden. "And the whole time, so many different aspects of the game are being worked on, especially ball-handling, passing, dribbling, rebounding, and shooting."

As soon as the defense gains possession of the ball, whether it be after a made or missed shot, or off a turnover, the defense becomes the offensive unit, and heads down the other end of the floor in search of a basket.

As soon as defense turns to offense, the group of five players on the opposite side of the floor gets ready to run out on defense. The first three players in this second group of five will burst off the line in exactly the same fashion as the first group of defensive players.

From there, the players begin a grueling rotation. Wooden explains that by using an odd number of players, the rotation never grows stale, as no three players will ever be a part of the same unit twice. He says that this drill provides a main objective for both the offensive and defensive teams.

"For the defensive team, the idea is never to give up the easy layup," says Wooden. "The defense must protect against the easy shot until they get help from that third defensive teammate, who evens up the numbers at three against three.

"As far as the offense goes," says Wooden, "the main objective is to get off a good shot, and not to force anything.

"In my entire coaching career, this drill covered more things than anything I ever came up with."

COACH'S CORNER

"THIS IS A BEAUTIFUL DRILL BECAUSE YOU ARE NOT ONLY LEARNING HOW TO DEFEND A THREE-ON-TWO BREAK, BUT YOU ARE LEARNING HOW TO ATTACK IN A THREE-ON-TWO SITUATION."

JOHN WOODEN, FORMER HEAD COACH, UCLA

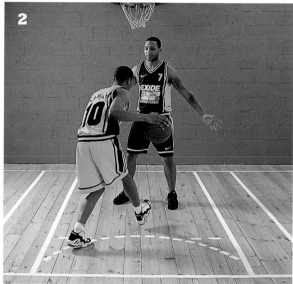

MR IBA DRILL

ob Evans, the former head coach at the University of Mississippi, now head coach for Arizona State, provides for this project what is perhaps the most grueling drill of all.

Coach Evans, formerly an assistant coach at Oklahoma State under Eddie Sutton, has continued to carry on a rugged exercise the two men affectionately called the Mr Iba Drill, named for Henry Iba, who coached at Oklahoma State from 1934 to 1970.

In setting up the Mr Iba Drill in his honor, Evans places one offensive man against one defensive man, and places himself on the court for additional assistance. The job of the offensive player in this drill is to take the ball directly at the defensive player, and the job of the defensive player is to intentionally stand in the way and draw a charge in the lane. Once the charge has been drawn, Coach Evans will roll another basketball toward either one

of the two sidelines. Despite just colliding with the offensive player and landing on the hardwood, the defensive player must quickly spring to his knees or his feet and dive for the loose ball that his coach has tossed out onto the floor.

There's more.

Once the defensive player has recovered the loose ball, he must secure it firmly to show possession, and then slip a quick pass back to his coach. Once he has released the pass, the defensive player will turn to offense, running into the paint, and taking a pass back from his coach.

Once he receives the return pass, the player in the paint must now try to score a basket, but in his way are two team managers or teammates who are holding out football-like tackle dummies and making intentional contact with the player in order to harass his scoring attempt. To complete this difficult drill, each player must score three baskets,

This sequence shows the type of charge players will face in the Mr Iba drill.

take one charge, dive for one loose ball, pass and catch the ball, and finally, fight his way through the tackle dummies three straight times or more, depending on how many shots that player needs to make three baskets. There is no time limit on this drill simply because it is declared over after each member of the team has taken his lumps.

"It's a draining exercise," says Evans. "But it teaches a player not to give up out there on the court. When Mr Iba coached, he loved tough players, and this is a real tough drill, so it's really a tribute to Mr Iba — our way of saluting him." This drill will get you ready for the court and toughen up your play for real game situations.

Working Overtime

THERE ARE A NUMBER OF TRADITIONAL SCHOOLYARD GAMES TO HELP A PLAYER HONE FUNDAMENTAL SKILLS OR EXPERIMENT WITH NEW MOVES. SOME COACHES EVEN INCORPORATE THAT SCHOOLYARD FUN INTO THEIR ORGANIZED PRACTICES. A PLAYER WILLING TO WORK OVERTIME ON HIS GAME MIGHT WANT TO MEMORIZE THE PAGES FROM THIS PART OF THE PLAYBOOK, WHICH ALSO INCLUDES MENTAL EXERCISES FROM A VERY DIFFERENT TYPE OF COACH.

BEAT THE PRO

Pick a spot on the floor, say 12 feet from the basket, and shoot from there. If you score, it's one point for you; if you miss, it's two points for say, Michael Jordan. First player to 10 points wins.

AROUND-THE-WORLD GOLF - PAR 49

A player must make seven shots from seven spots on the floor for a Par 49. As with golf, if Player A makes 49 baskets in 60 attempts while Player B makes 49 baskets in 55 attempts, then Player B wins because he netted 49 shots in five fewer attempts.

HORSE

A learning game. One player puts up a shot, maybe blindfolded or behind his back, that he doesn't think his opponent can match. If player A shoots and makes the basket, Player B must make the same basket. If Player B fails to make basket, he is charged with letter H. Both players take turns, and the first person who spells out H-O-R-S-E is the loser.

TWENTY-ONE

This game, perhaps the most popular played in schoolyards today, involves two or more players, and what makes this game so special is that, unlike the majority of other pickup games, it can be played with an odd number of players. Under the rules of Twenty-One, each player is his or her own team. The player in possession of the ball is on offense, and the rest of the players are on defense, teaming up to force a turnover or a missed shot, hoping to gain control of the ball for their own offensive possession.

A player who scores is awarded two points from the field, and then goes to the free-throw line. The player at the free-throw line can make as many as three free throws, which count as one point apiece, before regaining possession of the ball and attempting to score another two-point field goal. If the first, second, or third free throw is missed, one of the defensive players, or teams, will likely rebound the ball, become the offensive player, or team, and try to make his own two-point field goal, which in turn, will lead to a trip to the free-throw line. Of course, if the player shooting the free throw misses, he can very well grab his own rebound, and set himself up for another two-point field goal opportunity.

The object of the game is for the first player to reach a total of 21 points, and that player will be the winner. But wait, there's a catch. The winning twenty-first point needs to be made from a greater distance than the average 15-foot free throw. In most cases, the winning twenty-first point needs to travel the distance of a three-point shot, some 23

feet away from the basket. If this game-winning shot is missed, the player who missed must get back in the action, regain control of the ball and make another two-point field goal to earn another game-winning attempt.

Note: If a player has 20 points and makes a two-pointer, there is no bonus awarded. The idea is to get to 21. Passing 21 simply means earning the right to attempt the game-winning basket.

TWELVE-MAN DRILL

Tim Capstraw, the head coach at Wagner College in Staten Island, New York, likes to incorporate drills into his practices that resemble fun games more than exercises. One of Capstraw's favorite drills is a four-on-four defensive drill called the Twelve-Man Drill. To set up this exercise, Capstraw breaks 12 of his players into four groups of three. Working in a half-court set, Capstraw takes two of his groups and pits an offensive unit against a defensive unit.

At the whistle, the defensive unit is presented with the challenge of stopping the offense from scoring on three consecutive possessions in a 12-minute span. If, for example, the offense is stopped from scoring on its first possession but manages to score on the next, then the defensive unit will go back to trying for three consecutive stops. If this goal is reached, then the defensive unit gets to have some fun by playing offense, and making the next defensive unit sweat for a possible 12 minutes.

"The defensive teams can be out there for the entire 12 minutes sweating and working real hard, or they can get three quick stops and have fun playing offense," says Capstraw.

COACH'S CORNER

"THIS IS A VERY GOOD DRILL BECAUSE IT REALLY MOTIVATES THE DEFENSE TO STOP PEOPLE."

TIM CAPSTRAW, HEAD COACH, WAGNER COLLEGE, NEW YORK

SCORE AND STOP

Another fun drill that Tim Capstraw runs is a five-on-five, half-court or full-court drill he calls Score and Stop. In setting up this exercise, Capstraw places five offensive players against five defensive players and awards one point for the team who can score a basket and then turn around on defense and get a stop. The first team to a certain number of points, or to a greater number of points in a given time frame, will be declared the winners.

"Sometimes we'll just put ten minutes on the clock and let them play," says Capstraw. "In game situations, when teams score a basket, they tend to celebrate and allow the other team to come back and score. So here, we're taking pride in getting stops and not relaxing on defense.

"These drills might not be the prettiest," says Capstraw, "but they're the ones that work my kids' brains the best, and get us the best results."

SEVEN CHANCES

A third drill that Capstraw likes to use is called Seven Chances. In a half-court or full-court set, the five-player offensive unit will get seven opportunities to score against a five-player defensive set. When the seven chances are taken, the two units will switch sides of the ball, so that offense becomes defense and defense becomes offense. Again, the offensive unit will try to score as many baskets as it can in the space of seven possessions.

The team with more baskets will be declared the winner, while the losing team must endure some kind of punishment on the court, like the dreaded Suicide drill (see Chapter 1).

"The losers run," says Capstraw. "If you lose by one chance, you'll do one suicide. If you lose by two chances, we'll have you run two suicides.

"Believe me," says Capstraw, "these drills give the kids a lot of self-motivation."

TWO DRIBBLES IN A CIRCLE

Ray Rankis of Baruch College is one of the most respected coaches in the City University of New York Conference. He, too, believes in incorporating a certain element of fun and games into his sessions.

One of the drills that Rankis enjoys most is called Two Dribbles in a Circle. To set this game in motion, Rankis places two players in the middle of the jump circle at mid-court, each of those players holding a basketball. At the whistle, both players will begin dribbling the ball within the confines of the circle, and at the same time, each player will be using their free hand to try to knock the ball dribbled by the opposing player out of the circle.

"Both guys have to keep their dribble alive and the object is for one of them to knock the ball out of the other guy's hands while maintaining his own dribble," says Rankis, who basically uses this drill as a prepractice warm-up for his guards. "The player who does manage to knock his opponent's dribble out of the circle will score a point if the player who lost his dribble has to step out of the circle with both feet to pursue the basketball – the first player to score three points is declared the winner.

"Both players are really learning here how to protect the ball, and at the same time, they're learning ball-handling skills and how to keep their balance when they are attacking the ball," says Rankis. "Both players are on offense and defense at the exact same time, and both have the exact same goals."

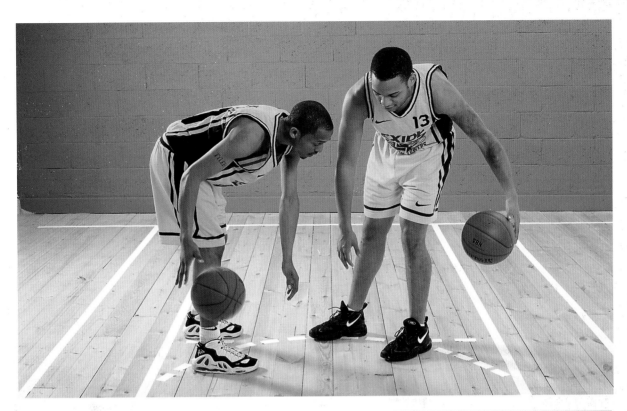

DRIBBLE TAG

Another fun drill that Ray Rankis's players love to run is called Dribble Tag, a game not much different than those that children in backyards and playgrounds have been playing for years.

To set up this drill, Rankis breaks his guards and big players up on each side of the court, and neither group is allowed to cross the mid-court line and join the other. Each player on the floor is holding a basketball. At the whistle, one player on each side of the half-court line who is declared "it" must run and try to tag one of his teammates while dribbling the basketball. The players who are trying to avoid being tagged are also dribbling basketballs. Once a player is tagged, he then becomes the dribbler who is chasing his teammates.

"We split them up because it will be too hard for the big guys to catch one of the little guys," says Rankis. "This is a great ball-handling drill because it requires dribbling with your right hand and left hand, speed dribbling, control dribbling and maneuvering to get away from each other."

TWENTY-SECOND SHOOT-OUT

Ray McCallum, the head coach at David Letterman's alma mater, Ball State University, likes to have a little fun of his own during practices. The one drill that McCallum turns into a competitive game concerns overall shooting.

"We do a lot of competition shooting with partners," said McCallum. "The key is to see how many shots you can make in a given amount of time." To set up this drill, McCallum separates his 12 players into groups of two-man teams, placing each of the teams at their own court.

Setting the clock at 20 seconds per man, and designating an area from which to shoot, McCallum will blow the whistle and each team will shoot for the highest number of baskets until time elapses. To give itself the best chance to win, each team will usually determine who is the better shooter of its two players, and who is the better rebounder. A good rebounder is crucial, since he will provide his shooter with more opportunities to score.

There are five areas of the floor where McCallum prefers his players to shoot jumpers from: the right baseline, left baseline, right-side free-throw line extended, left-side free-throw line extended, and the top of the key. When they are not shooting jumpers, McCallum will have his team take part in a free-throw shooting contest.

"It's important to practice shooting from everywhere on the court and to place an element of time pressure on the shooting," said McCallum. "Losers have to run sprints, and winners don't have to run at all. It's that simple."

Players who have trouble shooting free throws — like Shaquille O'Neal of the Los Angeles Lakers — or making shots from three-point range, or making left-handed layups, now have an opportunity to try to hone those skills with extremely unconventional drills as well as the numerous traditional exercises that appear in this book.

Arlene Berkman and Carol Ann Erickson of the Brain–Body Center For Performance Enhancement in Scarsdale, New York, say they can teach hoopsters a way of increasing their skill level through Educational Kinesology, a program they have designed to enhance brain function and movement.

"This is really unique because we are using movement to make the communication between the mind and the body," says Erickson. "When people are under pressure or stress, they do not access that ability to have everything cooking for them. We get the athlete in tune to what their bodies are telling them."

Here is a brief drill from the Brain-Body Center's program. These exercises are from the book *Brain Gym* by Paul E. Dennison (Ph.D). This series of exercises helps to prepare the athletes' focus and concentration, as well as the movement of their bodies, both at the same time. "If you think while you're moving out there, everyone is going by you," says Erickson, "take a golfer: if he thinks about the swing while he is swinging, there will be no rhythm to it."

According to Arlene Berkman, the director of the Brain-Body Center, Educational Kinesology can help the athlete accomplish several things: raise the player's level and consistency of play; help

1 **Drink a glass of water:** Drinking water increases energy, improves production and concentration (alleviates mental fatigue), and improves test-taking ability and all academic skills.

2 **Brain Buttons:** While holding the navel area with one hand, rub with thumb and finger of other hand in hollow areas (1 to 2 inches apart) under the collar bone on each side of the sternum (breastbone) just below the collar bone. By doing this, a person is increasing clarity for any visual activity or thinking skill.

3 **Cross-Crawl:** Touch hand to opposite knee, alternate moving one arm and opposite leg. Do this for 1–2 minutes with a variation – touch opposite elbow to knee. The cross-crawl exercise improves left–right coordination.

4 **Hook-Ups:** Put left ankle over right knee, left hand over ball of left foot (for some, right leg on top feels better). Sit this way for one minute, eyes closed, breathing deeply for another minute. Next, uncross legs, and put finger tips together, breathing deeply for another minute. Hook-Ups diffuses stress and promotes clear listening and speaking.

5 **Positive Points:** These points are just above the eyeballs, halfway between hairline and eyebrows. Lightly place three fingers of each hand together on those areas. Hold for 30–60 seconds. Alternative method: lightly hold hand across forehead. Positive Points decreases worrying and increases creative, constructive thinking.

the player to execute the playbook on the field; enhance the ability of the player to see the details and the whole field at the same time; help the players to see what their options are and make the best choice; give the player tools to help him maintain focus as the pressure of the game increases; and teach the athlete how to remain centered and calm under pressure.

"In a pressure or difficult situation in a game, an athlete may delay or have a lag in responding easily and efficiently on the court," says Erickson. "These stress patterns of movement can require unnecessary compensation in the body,

and over a period of time can lead to chronic injury and shorten their athletic career."

Erickson sums up the main objective of Educational Kinesology: "We're pinpointing the steps that are holding athletes back from what they are trying to do," she says. "And then using movement to stimulate their brain-to-body communication more efficiently. We're looking at the body as a whole, and how the whole body can be balanced and move more easily."

Brain Gym® is a registered trademark of the Educational Kinesology Foundation (Ventura, California, USA).

ACKNOWLEDGEMENT & DEDICATION

Just listening to Lenny Wilkens clear his throat taught me more about the game of basketball than I had ever known before. And how many people are fortunate enough, in a single lifetime, to talk X's and O's with other legends like John Wooden, Red Auerbach, Pete Carril, Lou Carnesecca and Jerry Tarkanian?

Thanks to all the other coaches who let me in on their huddles, especially Fran Fraschilla, a class act who spent more time with me than anyone else on this project.

Every time I glance at the boxscore, Elena Gustines is still the Most Valuable Player on my research team, always leading everyone else in assists. Thanks also to Nunyo DeMasio of the *Seattle Times*, who went ahead and challenged Gary Payton to a one-on-one without even finishing the game we started in New York, which I was leading 16-4 before the janitor turned the lights out.

A long overdue thanks to Julius Green, who always has me covered, and another thanks to Joe Brescia, whose basketball smarts made writing two books on the subject of hoops a whole lot easier.

If I could do it all over again, I'd stay young forever.

And so, this book is dedicated to the memory of my basketball youth, when I could still jump high enough to grab the rim. I miss the winter mornings on Pleasant Avenue, when Louis would ring the bell, and I'd look out the window to find him shovelling snow off

our favorite court. And to all those summer days we played in the park, from the time the sun rose high above the East River, long past the time it disappeared behind the old tenement buildings on the west side. I miss the rest of my team-mates, the guys I went to war with against all those kids from the projects: Austin, Christopher, Gregory, Ronald, James, Andrew, and Joe.

Kisses all around to my beautiful wife and best friend, Cathy, Mom and Dad, and the rest of the Mallozzi and Ammendolia clans.